# A Practical Guide to Analytics for Governments

# Wiley & SAS Business Series

The Wiley & SAS Business Series presents books that help senior-level managers with their critical management decisions.

Titles in the Wiley & SAS Business Series include:

*Analytics in a Big Data World: The Essential Guide to Data Science and its Applications* by Bart Baesens

*A Practical Guide to Analytics for Governments: Using Big Data for Good* by Marie Lowman

*Bank Fraud: Using Technology to Combat Losses* by Revathi Subramanian

*Big Data Analytics: Turning Big Data into Big Money* by Frank Ohlhorst

*Big Data, Big Innovation: Enabling Competitive Differentiation through Business Analytics* by Evan Stubbs

*Business Analytics for Customer Intelligence* by Gert Laursen

*Business Intelligence Applied: Implementing an Effective Information and Communications Technology Infrastructure* by Michael Gendron

*Business Intelligence and the Cloud: Strategic Implementation Guide* by Michael S. Gendron

*Business Transformation: A Roadmap for Maximizing Organizational Insights* by Aiman Zeid

*Connecting Organizational Silos: Taking Knowledge Flow Management to the Next Level with Social Media* by Frank Leistner

*Data-Driven Healthcare: How Analytics and BI are Transforming the Industry* by Laura Madsen

*Delivering Business Analytics: Practical Guidelines for Best Practice* by Evan Stubbs

*Demand-Driven Forecasting: A Structured Approach to Forecasting, Second Edition,* by Charles Chase

*Demand-Driven Inventory Optimization and Replenishment: Creating a More Efficient Supply Chain* by Robert A. Davis

*Developing Human Capital: Using Analytics to Plan and Optimize Your Learning and Development Investments* by Gene Pease, Barbara Beresford, and Lew Walker

*The Executive's Guide to Enterprise Social Media Strategy: How Social Networks Are Radically Transforming Your Business* by David Thomas and Mike Barlow

*Economic and Business Forecasting: Analyzing and Interpreting Econometric Results* by John Silvia, Azhar Iqbal, Kaylyn Swankoski, Sarah Watt, and Sam Bullard

*Economic Modeling in the Post Great Recession Era: Incomplete Data, Imperfect Markets* by John Silvia, Azhar Iqbal, and Sarah Watt House

*Foreign Currency Financial Reporting from Euros to Yen to Yuan: A Guide to Fundamental Concepts and Practical Applications* by Robert Rowan

*Harness Oil and Gas Big Data with Analytics: Optimize Exploration and Production with Data Driven Models* by Keith Holdaway

*Health Analytics: Gaining the Insights to Transform Health Care* by Jason Burke

*Heuristics in Analytics: A Practical Perspective of What Influences Our Analytical World* by Carlos Andre Reis Pinheiro and Fiona McNeill

*Human Capital Analytics: How to Harness the Potential of Your Organization's Greatest Asset* by Gene Pease, Boyce Byerly, and Jac Fitz-enz

*Implement, Improve and Expand Your Statewide Longitudinal Data System: Creating a Culture of Data in Education* by Jamie McQuiggan and Armistead Sapp

*Intelligent Credit Scoring: Building and Implementing Better Credit Risk Scorecards*, Second Edition, by Naeem Siddiqi

*Killer Analytics: Top 20 Metrics Missing from your Balance Sheet* by Mark Brown

*On-Camera Coach: Tools and Techniques for Business Professionals in a Video-Driven World* by Karin Reed

*Predictive Analytics for Human Resources* by Jac Fitz-enz and John Mattox II

*Predictive Business Analytics: Forward-Looking Capabilities to Improve Business Performance* by Lawrence Maisel and Gary Cokins

For more information on any of the above titles, please visit www.wiley.com.

# A Practical Guide to Analytics for Governments

*Using Big Data for Good*

**Marie Lowman**

WILEY

Published by John Wiley & Sons, Inc., Hoboken, New Jersey.
Published simultaneously in Canada.

For general information on our other products and services or for technical support, please contact our Customer Care Department within the United States at (800) 762-2974, outside the United States at (317) 572-3993 or fax (317) 572-4002.

Wiley publishes in a variety of print and electronic formats and by print-on-demand. Some material included with standard print versions of this book may not be included in e-books or in print-on-demand. If this book refers to media such as a CD or DVD that is not included in the version you purchased, you may download this material at http://booksupport.wiley.com. For more information about Wiley products, visit www.wiley.com.

*Library of Congress Cataloging-in-Publication Data:*

Names: Lowman, Marie, editor.
Title: A practical guide to analytics for governments : using big data for good / [edited by] Marie Lowman.
Description: Hoboken, New Jersey : John Wiley & Sons, Inc., 2017. | Series: Wiley & SAS business series | Includes index. |
Identifiers: LCCN 2017006645 (print) | LCCN 2017016282 (ebook) | ISBN 9781119362548 (pdf) | ISBN 9781119362852 (epub) | ISBN 9781119362821 (cloth)
Subjects: LCSH: Public administration—Statistical methods. | Public administration—Data processing. | Big data. | Data mining.
Classification: LCC JA71.7 (ebook) | LCC JA71.7 .P73 2017 (print) | DDC 352.3/8028557—dc23
LC record available at https://lccn.loc.gov/2017006645

Printed in the United States of America

10 9 8 7 6 5 4 3 2

# Contents

# Foreword

*Paula Henderson*

*Vice President, State and Local Government Practice, SAS Institute*

Nowhere can more good be done, for more people, than in government. Yes, that messy, challenging, and inspiring entity that simultaneously frustrates us and, often without us realizing it, dramatically improves our quality of life.

I lead a team of nearly 230 people whose mission is to help government, help people. It's our calling. Practically, we do that with software but, on a deeper level, we do it with passion, optimism, and a belief that analytics wielded by dedicated public servants is a force for good.

This book can empower those people to change lives. It is a guide to how analytics can address our country's most pressing issues. I also encourage regular citizens to read it. We all hear about analytics and big data but not everyone truly understands it. This book makes the application of data and analytics tangible, and builds excitement about the possibilities.

I have five children. The plight of at-risk kids in this country is never far from my mind. The all too frequent media stories detailing another preventable child fatality tear at my heart. I meet with government leaders on this topic. I serve on the board of a nonprofit dedicated to preventing child abuse. I evangelize the power of analytics to create brighter futures for children.

Will Jones contributes a chapter about improving child well-being by, in part, helping overburdened caseworkers prioritize risk to the children they're charged with protecting. The child protective services people I've met with consider it a sacred duty. But, we ask too much of them. No one understands that better than Will. He spent more than 20 years on the front lines of child protection, juvenile justice, and behavioral health.

That's what you need to understand about this book. It's not written by a bunch of PhD statisticians and data scientists. It's written by people who spent decades serving government at every level . . . serving you.

In addition to Will Jones, we have Nadja Young, a National Board Certified teacher with a passion for helping students succeed. She shares her inspirational and heartbreaking personal tale of how her life could have turned out much differently if not for dedicated teachers. This experience drives her efforts to assist state and local education agencies in better using data to improve student outcomes.

Jennifer Robinson, a town councilwoman for nearly 20 years, spends her days educating city and county leaders on the wide-ranging opportunities to be more efficient and serve their citizens more effectively with analytics. She believes the primary goal of Smart Cities should be to improve quality of life, and analytics is the foundation for those efforts. Her chapter is full of compelling and informative local government case studies.

Jeremy Racine has spent years evangelizing the use of prescriptive analytics, with positive patient outcomes as a top priority. He writes about how data and analytics offer unprecedented insight into skyrocketing healthcare costs and population health. This knowledge is key to unraveling the financial challenges and, more importantly, to combatting our most dire public health threats such as chronic disease, mental illness, and opioid abuse.

Opioid abuse is such a drastic problem, it warrants an entire chapter devoted to prescription drug abuse. As university faculty, a practitioner at Duke University Medical Center, and in 17 years at Pfizer Global Medial, Steve Kearney, PharmD, has seen every side of this issue. It's not just a public health issue, and not just a problem for law enforcement. Steve's helping agencies aid people in the throes of addiction, and put away those who profit illegally off the suffering of others.

David Kennedy has worked with criminal justice and public safety agencies for 12 years, helping them use data and analytics to manage cases, catch perpetrators, and keep citizens, and themselves, safe. But criminal justice challenges go well beyond getting bad guys off the streets. Prisons are overcrowded, recidivism rates are high, court systems are congested, and police–community relations are strained. David explains the role analytics can play.

Major General (Ret.) Jim Trogdon is a professional engineer with 30 years of experience in transportation, including five as chief operating officer at the North Carolina Department of Transportation. In January 2017 he was selected by Gov. Roy Cooper to lead that department. While we miss him at SAS, his expertise and leadership will be of even greater value to citizens of the Tar Heel State. He writes about getting people from point A to point B as safely and efficiently as possible with analytics. Oh, and I hope you're ready for autonomous vehicles.

A 26-year veteran of state government, Carl Hammersburg was a professional fraud buster for Washington State. He led data sharing and analytics efforts that doubled audits and tripled outcomes, earning awards from two successive governors. Fraud is rampant in government and manifests in unexpected places, perpetrated by sophisticated networks and schemes. Yes, Carl paints a bleak picture, but gives us hope, too.

When Kay Meyer led the creation of North Carolina's enterprise Government Data Analytics Center, she transformed the state's analytic approach to criminal justice, fraud, waste, compliance, and more. Now, she travels the country helping government agencies transform their states and localities by launching centers of analytics. When data sources that have never been integrated suddenly start talking to each other, it's amazing what can happen.

Our brave editor Marie Lowman has spent 20 years illuminating how technologies can help government agencies meet their goals. She gives this book the same treatment. Unable to resist the pull of public service, she served as an appointed commissioner for five years and is currently serving her second term as an elected councilmember.

Our country faces many problems. Literally, lives are at stake. Analytics can help, but its impact is intensified when used by people with a desire to make a difference. People like these authors. If you're reading this book, you're probably one of those people, too. I hope this book inspires you to consider ways to improve the lives of citizens through data and analytics. But, with or without software, we can all be a force for good.

# Acknowledgments

We would like to thank all of those who made this book possible, including our families, friends, colleagues, and SAS who supported us as we wrote the book. Thanks also go to Michelle Jozwiak, who helped us with graphics for the book, and Trent Smith for his writing support. We would also like to thank John Wiley & Sons for publishing the book in the Wiley and SAS Business Series and for providing superb assistance to us during the copyedit and production of the book.

CHAPTER **1**

# Introduction

*Marie Lowman*

The genius of big data is not only in the great number of new insights introduced, but even more in the new ideas for betterment these insights spawn. This paraphrase of Alexis de'Tocqueville's nineteenth-century observation of our democracy is still applicable today. Our government is expected to act as an honorable steward of our information and tax dollars. Stewardship, the responsible and careful management of something entrusted in one's care, demands that government demonstrate the effective and proper application of tax dollars to services and programs that provide the greatest benefit to its citizens.

Throughout my 21 years in the tech industry and eight-plus years serving in the public sector as an elected city council member and appointed commissioner, I have witnessed the increasing volume and velocity of data sources, and their overwhelming effect on government organizations—at times for the better, and at times, for the worse. The worse is when governments have no idea how to harness this data and use it for good. They make decisions with very little context, sometimes simply rendering a decision based on gut feelings alone. The better is when data is used as a catalyst to drive informed decision making, like the early identification of an at-risk child so a safe place can be provided for that child to stay while offering effective programs to support that child's growth to achieve their potential.

At every point of intersection between government and people, data is created. This data is being generated at an unprecedented rate, from an unprecedented number of sources. Data comes in all shapes and sizes: from citizens, law enforcement communities, businesses, other government entities, hospitals, utilities, roads, courts, prisons, and so on. Collecting this voluminous data enables government entities to better serve its citizens. The rate of data generated and collected daily has long since eclipsed humans' ability to analyze it, let alone identify and make use of *relevant* information. As governments confront the multitude of challenges around collecting and storing data, many are also grappling with how to extract meaningful insight from the data at their disposal.

Empowering government entities to collect meaningful data and then analyze and understand it in order to make better decisions is what I do for a living. It is a passion of mine. Governments must be able to separate the relevant from the insignificant, and the public from the confidential to ensure effectiveness and excellent stewardship. Analytics is the key to unlocking the true value hidden in this ever-growing data.

Committed government leaders dream  of making their communities stronger, more economically viable, safer, and better places to live and work. For some, leveraging analytics is making this dream a reality. Changing the way government views information technology (IT) and analytics requires dedication and persistent engagement. To make the case for analytics—and convince government and citizens of the need to change traditional business models, share data, and update IT infrastructures—government leaders must be able to show tangible beneficial evidence. They must be able to explain exactly how and why investment in analytics can save money, improve lives, avoid unnecessary future costs, and enhance operational efficiency and compliance. Many states have proven that the proper application and use of analytics can make governing more effective—by strengthening fraud detection, enhancing child welfare services, and improving health outcomes. They have shown that by applying analytics strategically, citizen services can be delivered faster and more cost effectively. See the graphic in the appendix to this book, Holistic Citizen Insight.

With sophisticated analytics, government leaders can pinpoint the underlying value in all their data. By bringing data together in a unified fashion they can see connections across agencies to better serve citizens. They can get an eye-opening, big-picture view that crosses cultural and political boundaries. They can understand not just what happened in the past, but why it happened and what is likely to happen next. Government leaders can begin to see what they need to do to make it happen again (if it was positive) or to prevent it (if it was negative).

The following chapters touch on several areas of government where analytics can make, and are making, a significant impact in the way governments operate. We highlight how putting analytics in play offers decision makers a holistic view from which they can make sound decisions—from one's childhood through their entire citizen lifecycle. Insights gleaned from early childhood into adulthood and from a broad range of government social and policy areas, offer a clearer picture of the many touch points government has with its citizens. This provides the ability to understand how our earliest encounters with a child can change trajectories and influence that child's future. Analytics enables insight about the interaction and interrelatedness of government programs to provide clear guidance around effective program performance, efficient government operations, and improved citizen quality of life. The following pages will take you on a journey from the very beginning.

## CHILD WELFARE

Our future begins with our children. We must protect, teach, and guide in an environment that will maximize every child's potential. Every child deserves a safe environment in which to grow. In many instances of child abuse or neglect, information is available that could help identify high-risk situations before tragedies occur. Analytics enable a broader, more comprehensive understanding of a child. Having a holistic view of a child enables better decision making about that individual child, and can help ensure he/she receives the best available services and care.

Analytics in play allows a practitioner to go beyond traditional risk assessment tools by incorporating quantitative capabilities that can help improve child safety. Important child-related information can be continually monitored and updated, and automated alerts can notify overworked and overburdened caseworkers whenever established thresholds are breached so they can intervene promptly to help keep children safe.

Valuable, timely information provided to caseworkers and managers enables them to proactively improve other program outcomes as well. Analytic insight can reduce child-support delinquencies, increase collections, and more efficiently manage hundreds of thousands of cases every year. Gaining a holistic view of a child offers his/her caregivers and service providers the ability to truly assist the child in reaching his/her potential. The establishment of a safe environment to grow is the foundation from which a child will learn. Through analytics our education system is gleaning vast insight to ensure every child's potential is realized.

## EDUCATION

Public schools are not only the foundation for a thriving economy, they are paramount to developing our greatest resource—human capital. How can we ensure a sustainable future of economic vitality and competitiveness in the purview of today's global society? Perhaps the most influential factor in the future of our economy is public education. Maintaining a globally competitive workforce begins in the classroom and educators must work creatively and effectively for impact. If our citizens and economies are to remain competitive, state leaders must implement policies and allocate resources to improve the effectiveness of the educational framework in public schools.

A successful education system flourishes in the harmonization of all factors that influence learning. Educators, environments, family backgrounds, health and other determinants all have a vital part to play in the success of a single student's education.

Transforming our nation's educational system requires accurate information to more precisely measure the impact of schools, programs, interventions, and teachers on student learning. Using data to understand both students' and teachers' strengths and weaknesses can guide implementing strategies that maximize the potential of both parties. The impact of this effort will lead our nation's schools toward real education transformation, and ultimately help establish the necessary foundation to boost our nation's economic prosperity. Like education, which lays the foundation for a vibrant economy, healthcare and the well-being of our citizens ensures their quality of life—but also represents one of the greatest challenges in terms of cost and service delivery.

## HEALTHCARE

Analytics have become a vital underpinning to Medicaid managed care policy and program administration. In April 2016, the Centers for Medicare and Medicaid Services (CMS) released the first major update to Medicaid managed care in more than 10 years. A decade can bring about a lot of change. A unique opportunity for more comprehensive, advanced analytics for quality of care improvement, value-based care, program and fiscal integrity, and better management of the Medicaid managed care program is upon us. There are many factors contributing to the breakneck speed with which healthcare costs are rising. Using analytics to identify critical factors offers a mechanism for putting the right pressure on the brakes. Of significant concern is the rampant rise in opiate abuse. This epidemic is hampering first responders' and healthcare providers' ability to meet emergency demand, and is having a crippling fiscal impact.

## PRESCRIPTION DRUG ABUSE

Opiate abuse is rising to unprecedented levels, and its abuse is not limited or contained by geographic boundaries. A combination of factors has contributed to the surge in heroin use, including economics (heroin is cheaper than many drugs), a crackdown on prescription painkillers and methamphetamine, and a lack of resources for intensive, effective treatment programs. The toll heroin takes on our communities is undeniable.

Financial costs for law enforcement and public safety agencies, social services programs, child welfare, and the healthcare system have skyrocketed in tandem with the increase in addiction—not just to heroin, but to many substances. Most importantly, the emotional and mental toll heroin takes on families and friends is devastating. Analytics can significantly enhance efforts related to identifying those most at risk for addiction by enabling early, effective intervention.

Introducing advanced analytics can help prescription drug monitoring programs improve upon their success by proactively identifying diversion via multiple provider episodes, inappropriate prescribing, and development of indicators to distinguish between individuals who are abusing prescription drugs and those who are criminally diverting them for profit. Addressing opiate abuse with effective intervention strategies can help alleviate the increased burden on law enforcement tasked with the protecting the public.

## CRIMINAL JUSTICE AND PUBLIC SAFETY

Law enforcement personnel place their lives on the line every day to keep our communities safe, to protect and serve, and to safeguard the freedoms and liberties afforded by our country. They are tasked with making split-second decisions that can, and often do, have a profound impact on those involved and the public at large.

It is a challenging time for the U.S. criminal justice and public safety system. Prisons are overcrowded, recidivism rates are high, court systems are congested, and police–community relations are strained. Access to information coupled with real-time analyzed data must be available to those making the decisions. Forward-thinking policymakers and law enforcement personnel rely on data supported by analytics to help them make improvements to current processes based on today's challenges, today's data, and today's best options. Criminal justice and public safety agencies can change outcomes and impact lives via the use of data and analytics.

## SMART CITIES

A smart city is an ecosystem where technological solutions facilitate sustainable economic growth and resource efficiency, with the ultimate goal of improving the quality of life of all citizens.

Sensor data, combined with traditional data sources, benefit from technologies that offer real-time decision making, development of rapid analytical models, simulations, predictive analytics, and optimization. Analyzing this voluminous data enables cities to better serve their citizens by presenting the collected data in a highly understandable format for citizens. Traffic alerts, parking availability, retail water usage, and crime reporting are just a few of the many ways citizen intelligence is enhanced. A smart city effectively uses information and communications technology (ICT) to enhance its livability, workability, and sustainability.

## TRANSPORTATION

Information and communications technology has strengthened the states' Departments of Transportation's ability to improve road safety, save money through better, more efficient decision making, and enhance the overall transportation network. A better understanding of where roads should be constructed while taking into consideration environmental features, improving the quality of the road itself, and implementing maintenance procedures at the right time in the right place have all contributed to bottom-line savings for transportation departments. With the introduction of sensor technology, autonomous and connected vehicles have the potential to transform personal mobility while generating vast quantities of data to significantly improve safety, improve transportation network performance, reduce congestion, improve freight flows, enhance transportation finance, and improve quality of life.

## FRAUD, WASTE, AND ABUSE

All government programs are vulnerable to fraud, waste, and abuse. Government fraud is at an all-time high and growing rapidly. Industry research shows that all together, fraud, waste, and abuse represent about 10 percent of overall government program spending. It's making budget deficits bigger—and forcing elected officials to close deficit gaps by either raising taxes or eliminating programs. Neither option is ideal. What if governments could minimize deficits by eliminating fraud, waste, and abuse? Forward-looking government leaders are already acting by implementing enterprise-level, state-of-the-art fraud detection programs designed to keep pace with increasingly sophisticated perpetrators.

There are several areas where combating fraud, waste, and abuse in government programs can reap big benefits. In the tax and revenue arena, analytics can help close the tax gap with more effective audits and investigations by predicting fraud and noncompliance, and finding suspicious activity quickly. Within workforce programs, analytics can assist with diagnosing the eligibility and legitimacy of claims in unemployment and workers' comp programs—including employee misclassifications— by analyzing disparate sources of data. Looking at benefits program's governments can save billions by moving beyond pay and chase for Medicare, Medicaid, SNAP, TANF, and so on. An integrated workflow offers the ability to analyze data from multiple sources to detect potential fraud in near real time across the entire government enterprise.

## ESTABLISHING A CENTER OF ANALYTICS

Putting analytics in play across the entire government enterprise just may be the Holy Grail. Greater IT efficiency, better use of human capital, and smarter decision making are where we all win. The establishment of a center for analytics, that leverages all available data sources in the most efficient, cost-effective manner, is where we all can experience the rewards of great decision making. Analytics is the key to unlocking valuable insight.

A unique aspect of government is that really, at the end of the day, it does what all private entities do—combined. Governments perform banking and financing functions, economic development functions, travel and tourism functions, service delivery, healthcare, the list goes on. For government, there are lessons to be learned and best practices from which to capitalize with the rapid adoption of analytics in the private sector.

On a daily basis I engage in fascinating conversations with my colleagues, most of whom have dedicated some part of their careers to working in the public sector as practitioners of their respective fields. Their collective knowledge is not only inspiring, but a treasure trove for those who have found the key and are able to unlock it. This book is meant to be that key, unlocking a wealth of domain expertise, practical application, knowledge, and experience. It is my goal that this book will serve as a guide for policymakers, legislators, staffers, government leaders, government employees, and, perhaps most importantly, citizens, to better understand how putting analytics at the forefront of the decision-making process can enable us all to not only know better, but to do better.

Throughout the following pages you'll find we've pulled together some of our favorite best practices that showcase the role analytics plays in better decision making. This compilation is not meant to be exhaustive—we are just getting started! These chapters provide in-depth discussions of the issues at hand, explore the ways analytics can help address those issues, and have real-world examples of how government entities are embracing analytics and doing better as a result—a result where we all win.

To apply Maya Angelou's popular adage to our topic at hand, when governments know better, they can do better. Better policymaking occurs, more effective legislation is enacted, targeted programs and services are appropriately directed to those who most need the assistance, and we can sleep well knowing our taxpayer dollars are being utilized to their fullest potential.

**PROFILE**

**Marie Lowman** is a Principal Industry Consultant—Government at SAS Institute. For over 21 years, Lowman has overseen SAS's commitment to helping government organizations provide high-quality services to their constituents, while maximizing resources and budgets. Ms. Lowman served for more than 5 years as an appointed planning and zoning commissioner and currently serves as an elected council member for the city of Bee Cave, Texas. She holds a BS and an MS from Indiana University and an MBA from Meredith College.

CHAPTER **2**

# Child Well-Being

*Will Jones*

# INTRODUCTION

I often get asked the question by friends and colleagues of why I decided to leave the human services industry to work for an analytics software and solutions company. Interestingly enough, this is not a question that causes me to pause and reflect upon my 23 years of human services work in both the public and private sectors in which I have seen a lot of positive change and improved outcomes in many areas. On the other hand, I have seen little or no change in many areas despite significant advancements in research, science, and technology. In a word, my answer is impact. I have been extremely fortunate to witness how data utilization can change the trajectory of how both private and public human services organizations can actually stop being simply reactive, and begin to take an innovative, proactive approach to help solve complex problems. I actually believe in my core that I never left human services, but have simply taken a position that will allow me to have both a deeper and wider impact on the number of at-risk children and families as I work to educate those influencing and working in state and local government human services to approach problems and solutions differently. Unfortunately, government often finds it difficult to introduce and embrace change and innovation despite the potential positive impact.[1]

Children in America are still struggling to enjoy the quality of life they deserve, and many are suffering. Twenty-two percent of American children are living in poverty (an increase from previous years); more than 3 million reports of child abuse are made in the United States involving over 6 million children; we are losing an average of 4 to 7 children per day due to child abuse and/or neglect-related deaths; and 17.5 million children are being served through child-support services.[2]

We keep doing the same things over and over and expect different outcomes. Albert Einstein would refer to it as insanity, but many youth services professionals refer to it as business as usual. I am exaggerating a bit—there have been some pockets of true innovation and change, but they have been limited at best. Despite good intentions, the government continues to struggle to get a clear picture of which services children are receiving, and to assess their impact on improving child outcomes in an effort to identify which service or combination of services have the best chance of helping to stop the cycle of violence, poverty, and joblessness. Human services agencies as a whole are data rich, but analysis poor. We now know that data can be leveraged and analyzed more effectively to provide greater insight into the past, the present, and the future.

This chapter will highlight why data analytics should begin to be seen as an untapped resource and tool that can actually allow human services to be proactive rather than reactive in addressing the needs of youth and families involved in services, as well as a plethora of increasing workforce issues from high turnover, tools and resources, to worker safety. That being stated, it is imperative that organizations focus on culture to ensure that data-driven decision making and results-oriented accountability help establish a firm foundation.

## DATA-DRIVEN CULTURE

I remember when I first started in public human services 23 years ago and the word *outcomes* was introduced. At that time, we believed that if it felt good and children and families seemed happy that we were doing a good job—those were our outcomes. We were wrong. We now know the differences between outputs and outcomes and the importance of measuring multiple indicators to determine positive results and identify areas of improvement, but many public and private sector youth service organizations still do not track, measure, or react to outcomes.

In addition, many visualize data, but do nothing to analyze it further to determine why outcomes may be moving in the right or wrong directions. Unfortunately, this makes it extremely difficult to replicate practices that work or identify why something is not working. A recent example of this was highlighted in a report generated by the Alaska Department of Juvenile Justice showing that the number of kids being sent their way is almost half what it was 10 years ago (see Figure 2.1). Despite having access to historical data, it was cited that "the reason behind the decrease isn't completely clear, but it's a nationwide trend."[3] This is actually the rule, not the exception. Many state human services organizations are using data to inform them of how they are doing or what they are doing, but currently cannot lean on their data to answer why, which limits the actual

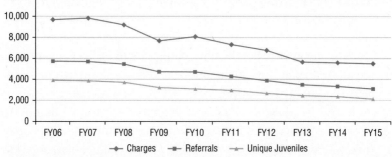

| Fiscal Year | FY06 | FY07 | FY08 | FY09 | FY10 | FY11 | FY12 | FY13 | FY14 | FY15 |
|---|---|---|---|---|---|---|---|---|---|---|
| Charges | 9,700 | 9,834 | 9,200 | 7,692 | 8,062 | 7,310 | 6,751 | 5,655 | 5,617 | 5,501 |
| Referrals | 5,713 | 5,709 | 5,443 | 4,697 | 4,678 | 4,261 | 3,859 | 3,462 | 3,309 | 3,083 |
| Unique Juve | 3,929 | 3,876 | 3,728 | 3,224 | 3,101 | 2,945 | 2,664 | 2,462 | 2,385 | 2,118 |
| Charges per | 1.70 | 1.72 | 1.69 | 1.64 | 1.72 | 1.72 | 1.75 | 1.63 | 1.70 | 1.78 |

Charge/Offense is used to designate an individual violation of the law or an offense. A delinquency Referral is a request by a law enforcement agency for a DJJ response following the arrest of a juvenile or as a result of the submission of a police investigation report alleging the commission of a crime or violation of a court order. A referral is counted as a single episode or event. Some referrals include more than one charge. Juveniles represent the number of unique juveniles who were referred to DJJ during the fiscal year. Some juveniles were referred multiple times within the year.

**Figure 2.1** Past Crime Rates Give Perspectives on Lower Juvenile Detention Numbers
*Source: Quinton Chandler, Alaska Public Media, September 6, 2016.*

power of data. Analytics actually exposes the power of human services data to begin providing valuable insights into the population served that can answer the why questions and allow organizations to be forward thinking in their approach to impact.

One ex–state commissioner and child welfare expert recently stated, "Predictive analytics is the future of success in child welfare." Is the concept of predictive analytics today what outcomes was 22 years ago? If so, I hope that the field is prepared to act much quicker to improve services to children and families, proactively reform, and increase positive outcomes for our most vulnerable population. There is tremendous potential for child welfare agencies to use vast stores of data to improve outcomes for children and families. Despite being rich in data, many agencies have yet to establish the data-driven culture that's required to advance both practice and policy.

Given the fact that the industry is data rich but analysis poor, now is the time for administrators and policymakers to lean on the power of analytics in an effort to do things differently and expect different and improved outcomes. It is critical that organizations understand the importance of developing and nurturing a culture that embraces data collection, analysis, and utilization to inform decision making at every level of the organization.

There is currently a consensus among analytics consultants that few organizations have developed the culture needed to maximize the utilization of data to truly impact those that are served. In a recent interview with Jerry Milner of the Center for Support of Families, he stated, "A lot of social workers will say, 'I'm not interested in the data; I want to work with children and families.' To change that attitude, the data has to be relevant to the people who will use it. They have to understand that the numbers are representative of the children and families they're serving. The greatest data and analytics in the world won't have any effect if they don't fuel a decision or change something. That requires a culture where people understand, value, and demand fact-based decisions and strategies."

What happened to the adage, "What gets measured, gets done?" Though progress is being made, there are too many child protection agencies that have yet to understand the profound impact data-informed policy and practice have on performance outcomes, as well as staff retention and satisfaction. I have the unique opportunity to have conversations around data-driven management and case practice all over the United States, and I continue to be told that organizations have limited real-time data at their fingertips to help guide decisions on a daily basis. I am not referencing advanced analytics, but simple dashboards that provide insight into the health of a system to ensure that things are moving in the right direction. If human services' leaders are not leaning on their data, what are they leaning on to make the best informed decisions possible?

Without dipping deep into the well, I pulled this small sample of quotes from multiple reports and audits done on state and local government child-serving agencies that reflect the rule, not the exception:

> Staff stated there is a need for analytical support to extract data and create reports, which would provide better information regarding call information for management to staff appropriately for peak times.[4]

> The Child Abuse and Neglect Center Referrals Statistical Summaries do not include data on After Hour Program calls nor average number of calls and dispositions per social worker, to provide adequate information to manage staffing.[5]

> Over the course of the audit, department staff routinely indicated they recognize CPS activities are not well documented. However, they stress their work keeps children safe and ultimately that is the focus of their activities, with documentation of those activities being secondary.[6]

> The Department is data rich, but analysis poor. They do not use data to in assessing, planning, implementing, evaluating, and improving the effectiveness of service delivery.[7]

No one would ever say we should put data collection over child safety, but it doesn't have to be an either/or decision. In fact, better data analysis will help caseworkers know where best to spend their limited time to have the most impact and will also help those in leader-ship not only identify problems, but also the cause of those problems that will help better inform actions and countermeasures that will help ameliorate performance issues.

Some agencies are further along than others, but many lack the tools, capacity, and data-driven culture to implement business report-ing and/or advanced analytics into continuous quality-improvement efforts. It all starts with laying a firm foundation within the culture of the agency that emphasizes data collection, analysis, and utilization of data to improve the ability to make informed case practice and policy decisions.

## DATA SHARING

Unfortunately many times change is a result of a compelling incident or string of incidents. This doesn't have to be the case. We should not have to wait for something tragic to happen to begin to implement solutions that we already know are needed and will add value. Sharing across welfare and other government agencies is seen as key to stopping abuse before it's too late. I recently co-presented at a conference with a state director of public health who was speaking to data sharing when he stated, "One of the greatest problems we have is institutional jealousy." Although many governments have begun to break down the barriers of data sharing between agencies for quality of life outcomes, most are not yet there. This is not a technology issue, but a policy and procedure issue that must be overcome to truly impact our most vulnerable populations. Recently, a spike in child abuse cases in New Zealand has caused the Ministry of Social Development to reexamine data sharing: "The Social Development Minister, Anne Tolley, says a child's life is critical, but social service workers, health workers and non-government organizations don't swap information because they're scared of breaking privacy laws. 'What we know is that sometimes when the information starts to come to the table it's been clear that actually people have had information earlier on and not shared,' said Sue Macklin of the Ministry of Social Development. So the Government plans to change the law to reassure professionals. 'We need to flip it on [its] head and say what's is more important and then how do we protect you when you share that information in good faith,' Mrs Tolley said."[8]

Data can also be used to help ensure worker safety. A Vermont Department of Children Families worker was murdered in early 2016. The lead suspect is the mother of a child who was previously removed from her care and placed in foster care. This tragedy illustrates the challenges and risks that workers have in the field of serving at-risk youth.

I have seen many things. I was threatened by an irate stepfather with a handgun in my first year of employment. I've been threatened by teenage youths in the juvenile justice system who I was trying to help. I was exposed to the aftermath of a major traumatic event where a client murdered his counselor and another client, then committed suicide in front of other agency staff. I saw my pregnant wife, a former Child Protective Services worker, visit parents of children in foster care with little information about their criminal or social history, or the environment she would enter. As an administrator, I witnessed numerous threats to my staff.

The tragedy in Vermont is not the first, just one of the more recent. I can only hope that the youth services field takes an opportunity to grieve appropriately, then takes action to help the first responders be better equipped to deal with potentially threatening incidents.

It is imperative that employees who do this work be supported by providing them needed supervision, tools, training, and an organization's culture that makes staff safety paramount, not secondary, which includes improving the amount of information readily available to a field worker. By integrating data and making it available in a usable format we can improve the quality and amount of information a worker has. This includes information about the child, family, and other parties to the case, directly or indirectly involved, as well as the environment where they reside.

This will greatly assist in identifying potential risk as workers engage children, parents, and other family members. This can be done, but must become top of mind for state and local government agencies, as well as those in the private sector. I would encourage first responders to appropriately challenge their leadership to make staff safety a priority, and not another initiative in the queue.

Despite the ongoing concerns around privacy, many jurisdictions are beginning to understand the value of integrating data for social good and more are moving in that much needed direction.

## DATA QUALITY

As an ex–child welfare administrator, I often had to be involved in case staffings where critical decisions were being made as to the direction of a case, from closing supervision to termination of parental rights. Every decision is critical and could impact both the short- and long-term impact of a child's safety, well-being, and permanency. I have always been asked about how I made those types of life-and-death decisions. My response automated as I felt good about decisions that I help make given the fact that I believed that I was making the best informed decision I could make given the information available to me at the time of the staffing. I still believe that I made the best decisions that could have been made given the information I had available to me, however, I now understand that there is information and data within case management systems that is not being made available to those making the same life-and-death decisions.

In a recent analytic assessment conducted by SAS of the Florida Department of Children and Families, using data over a 10-year

Initial inspections data has revealed unique persons in SACWIS assigned to multiple Person IDs. To get a complete picture and history of a person, the first analytic task was to consolidate these multiple representations into a single unique person called a "Key ID" (KID).

**Figure 2.2** Key ID (KID)

history, it was identified that the number-one predictor of future maltreatment, including fatality, of a child is intergenerational abuse history. We also know that case-management systems have a robust amount of case history, but data quality limits the ability to surface all historical information needed to help workers make the most informed decision possible as it related to child safety. Currently, *they don't know what they don't know.*

An initial inspection of the data revealed unique persons in the case management system assigned to multiple person IDs. To get a complete picture and history of a person, the first analytic task was to consolidate these multiple representations into a single unique person called a Key ID (KID; Figure 2.2).

In addition, a better understanding of the relationships between a given child and others in the child's event history to help inform of potential risk factors became evident. To ensure that a complete history could be made available to help inform decisions, entity resolution was performed across three layers or relationships to enable them to connect all of the dots. These included:

1. Previous reports and intakes for a selected child.
2. Previous reports and intakes for those in the same cases as the selected child.
3. Previous reports and intakes for those linked to the cases of the selected child but not including the selected child.

To demonstrate the impact and added value of this type of analytics, Figure 2.3 shows a real-life case study of a child-death case without

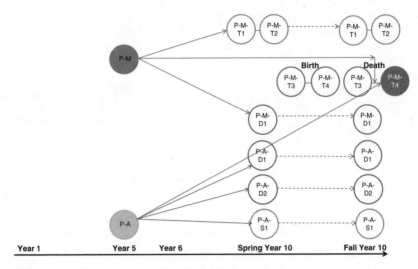

**Figure 2.3** Case Study: Without Entity Resolution

entity resolution, while Figure 2.4 shows the exact same case following the entity resolution process across the three layers of relationship. Here, one case study is presented to show the extent of the maltreatment cycle and the complexity of relationships in the child welfare system. The case illustrated had one fatality occur in the fall of year 10, when an infant almost four months old died. The death was recorded due to neglect and inadequate supervision and the cause of the death was sudden unexpected infant death.

The fatality report in the fall of year 10 showed three perpetrators—the mother (P-M), the grandmother (GM), and an aunt (P-A). The deceased child (P-M-T4) had a twin sister (P-M-T3) and in addition to the twin infants, the mother had another infant daughter (P-M-D1) and another twin who were almost two (2) years old (P-M-T1 and P-M-T2). Deceased child was born earlier in Year 10. At the time of the death, open cases also included the grandfather (GF) and five other siblings of the grandparents (D1, D2, S1-S3) as well as a child of one other aunt (D1-D) and three children of the perpetrator aunt (P-A-D1, P-A-D2, P-A-S1) who was married to one of the uncles (S3). All children in the case, four kids of the perpetrator mother and three children of the perpetrator aunt, were recorded as victims in the fatality report.

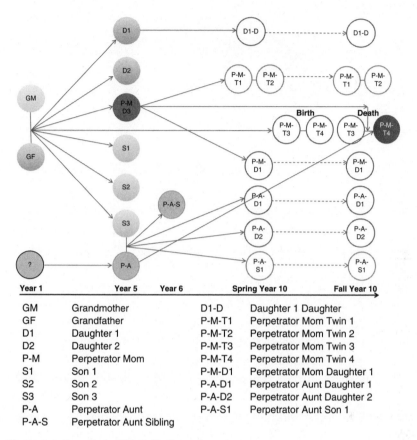

| GM | Grandmother | D1-D | Daughter 1 Daughter |
| GF | Grandfather | P-M-T1 | Perpetrator Mom Twin 1 |
| D1 | Daughter 1 | P-M-T2 | Perpetrator Mom Twin 2 |
| D2 | Daughter 2 | P-M-T3 | Perpetrator Mom Twin 3 |
| P-M | Perpetrator Mom | P-M-T4 | Perpetrator Mom Twin 4 |
| S1 | Son 1 | P-M-D1 | Perpetrator Mom Daughter 1 |
| S2 | Son 2 | P-A-D1 | Perpetrator Aunt Daughter 1 |
| S3 | Son 3 | P-A-D2 | Perpetrator Aunt Daughter 2 |
| P-A | Perpetrator Aunt | P-A-S1 | Perpetrator Aunt Son 1 |
| P-A-S | Perpetrator Aunt Sibling | | |

**Figure 2.4** Case Study: With Entity Resolution

The deceased child did not have an earlier report (level 0). However, there were two earlier reports in spring of year 10 when the mother was recorded as a perpetrator and her older three children as victims. Similarly in these reports, the grandmother and the aunt were recorded as perpetrators and children of the aunt as victims. The child of the other aunt was also a victim. These reports also included the grandfather as a perpetrator.

The cases become even more complex when tracking these families back to earlier years. In year 6, a report recorded the perpetrator aunt and her husband as perpetrators where the victim is the younger sibling of the aunt. Then between years 1 and 5, one can observe several counts of alleged maltreatments that involved multiple members of these families.

|  | Without Entity Resolution | With Entity Resolution |
|---|---|---|
| Report History Count | 44 | 127 |
| Intergenerational Abuse History | NO | YES |
| Risk Percentile | 82.7 | 99.6 |

**Figure 2.5** Intergenerational History and True Risk

The grandmother and grandfather were recorded as perpetrators several times, maltreating their six children including the perpetrator mother. Hence, mother appeared as a victim in her earlier life. Similarly, the perpetrator aunt was abused multiple times together with her sibling by her family between years 1 and 5. Hence, both the aunt and her husband were abused in the past and they became perpetrators for their own children in the future.

After counting all roles, at the time of the fatality event, the total number of report histories for the deceased child was 127. There were also two perpetrators as victims (mother and the aunt) and many counts of intergenerational maltreatment. Report histories and perpetrator-as-victim counts are the two strongest predictors in the model. As you can see in Figure 2.5, once the data-quality issues have been resolved, intergenerational history, as well as true risk, become more evident.

## ASSESSING RISK

As state and local government leaders and community advocates explore how they can use predictive analytics to analyze data to improve child well-being outcomes, many questions have surfaced. For years, government youth services agencies across the United States used actuarial risk and need assessment tools. These technologies use predictive analytics to identify static risk factors that indicate potential problems. Although these tools are a good starting point, many problems are associated with their implementation, such as required fidelity, worker bias, amount of time to complete, and so on. In a recent article titled "How Big Data Can Help Save Endangered Lives,"[9] following the death of a six-year-old boy in New York City, it was suggested that big data might be a solution. Big data is not a solution, but should definitely be part of the solution based on what we currently know. The same article included an interview with Richard Gelles, former dean of the School of Social Policy and Practice at the University of Pennsylvania, who stated, "Even the state-of-the-art assessment tools being used in New York are no better at predicting risk for a child than if you flipped a coin." Gelles says social workers using clinical judgment and their own expertise to determine which children should be removed from their homes is simply inadequate.

A more operational analytics approach for risk assessment uses both static and dynamic risk factors to calculate the risk of maltreatment. More timely dynamic data increases accuracy, improves scoring, and limits worker bias.

In early December 2015, two children, ages three and seven, were found dead in a locker in a small Monterey County, California community.[10] When I first heard about it, I said to myself, "This may be one of the worst cases of child abuse that I have ever been a part of or heard about in the past 21 years." That is saying a lot considering that I have worked in child welfare during that entire time and have been directly and indirectly exposed to many bad cases. Unfortunately, I could not help myself in becoming a bit of an armchair quarterback by asking what could have been done differently. Were there opportunities to identify risk early to allow for a proactive action? What improvements can be made in policy and practice to prevent this in the future?

My initial curiosity was piqued early on when the media shared that there had been multiple prior engagements by the county's department of social services and local law enforcement. As someone who may not be considered green anymore, I understand that what is in the media is only a third of the story, so I waited. In January 2016, a few months after the incident and media frenzy that highlighted this horrific case, the California Department of Social Services (CDSS) completed a Critical Incident Review of this case as well as a sampling of cases worked by the county in question during the same period of time. I applaud Monterey County Department of Social and Employment Services (MCDSES) as well as CDSS for the level of transparency provided and that resulted in this report.

A few critical takeaways from the report include, but are not limited to:[11]

- MCDSES generated five referrals involving the children and aunt in the critical incident.
- MCDSES received a suspected child abuse report that was not opened or investigated as a new referral.
- In one referral, MCDSES did not immediately complete the protocol or conduct an in-person investigation, but relied on information provided by law enforcement who conducted a welfare check.
- In one referral, one child disclosed physical abuse to themselves and another child that was not documented as an additional allegation in the system.
- In three referrals, the Structured Decision Making (SDM) actuarial hotline tool was not completed as required. In two referrals, SDM safety and risk assessments were not completed timely, and in one referral, the SDM safety and risk assessment was completed based on incomplete information about the conditions of the home.
- Eight of 24 referrals and cases demonstrated that the SDM hotline tool was not completed timely as required.
- Twenty-two of 24 referrals and cases reviewed did not demonstrate documentation that investigative staff independently reviewed the family's prior history, which is inconsistent with best practice.
- Safety and risk assessment tools aid a social worker in identifying whether a child can safely remain in their home and must be done when the worker has reached a conclusion regarding continuing services. Per the review, 75 percent of SDM tools were not completed timely per protocol.

The above statements are consistent with similar reports in similar jurisdictions across the country in the past two years when reviewing remaltreatment and fatality cases involving children with prior involvement with the child welfare system, yet there seems to be a hesitancy to change and be open to new approaches to assess and react to risk.

Actuarial tools based on predictive factors is a good start, but they have not been proven to be a good finish. Unfortunately, turnover and tenure in the industry make it difficult to ensure consistency and fidelity in assessing risk and safety for children. In addition, it allows for worker and system bias to be inserted while worker judgment may not be what it used to be due to the constant turnover and change. The case in question is a direct reflection of this. Where do we go from here to be much more proactive and truly impact outcomes?

Information from actuarial tools, institutional knowledge, and data from current case management systems can be used to create a validated operational analytic assessment of risk and safety that is designed to accurately identify case information that may be critical for identifying potential for re-maltreatment. This can fill many of the gaps already identified by:

- Automating daily assessments of risk and safety.
- Alerting workers, supervisors, and administrators of high-risk cases.
- Creating unique person IDs or KIDs to help ensure that all the possible data and historical information about kids is available to inform decisions. There is a high likelihood that an initial inspection of the data would reveal unique persons in their case management system assigned to multiple person IDs.
- Accounting for the relationship of factors that increase and decrease risk and informing the worker accordingly.
- Eliminating worker bias.

My hope is that we learn from tragic incidents such as this and truly embrace innovation and change rather than look for reasons to not try things differently.

## ADDRESSING THE PERCEIVED LIMITS OF ANALYTICS PERTAINING TO ASSESSING RISK

As government leaders and community advocates look to advanced analytic approaches to refine the delivery of human services, they often meet barriers from those who are unclear on how analytics works—and what it can deliver. These misperceptions typically fall into one of four areas:

1. False positives
2. Racial bias and disparity
3. Equation versus comprehensive process
4. Beliefs that current, nonanalytics tools are sufficient

**Misperception 1: Analytics will yield a high number of false positives, giving workers added work.**

Child-safety models use a multitude of risk factors that vary in complexity. These aren't just yes/no responses. Risk factors are intuitive. By factoring in the conditions of thousands of cases and their environment, analytics can determine a child's situation when facing similar risk factors. For example, analytics can mine prior maltreatment allegations by the child's primary caregivers.

To be in the highest-risk segments, a child needs to have extreme values in a multitude of risk factors. When identified, the risk of general harm to a child is also elevated, not just the risk of fatality. And the modeling for fatalities is traditionally focused on just fatal events. Analytics can help take into account other significant events (for example, a child ends up in ICU due to abuse) to help provide a more accurate picture of the situation.

With this information driving the analytics, the risk can increase and decrease given all of these factors. SAS Analytics helps identify cases that are at increased risk, allowing for mitigation earlier than before. As risk factors decrease (from a change in the child's living arrangement or some other factor), the analytics can adjust recommendations accordingly.

Analytics helps child advocates more accurately find cases that require intervention. SAS for child safety typically identifies less than 5 percent of overall cases as being at the highest level of risk of maltreatment and/or fatality. As a comparison, current validated actuarial risk and needs assessments routinely identify from 25 to 30 percent of cases as being high to very high risk of maltreatment—a difference in false positives of up to 500 percent.

**Misperception 2: Predictive analytics can introduce racial bias and disparity within communities.**

Racial disparity is not apparent in fatalities or maltreatment. Predictive analytic models in multiple jurisdictions have found no significant difference in maltreatment and/or fatality risk for black versus white households. This race effect, while statistically significant, is eclipsed by other risk factors like prior maltreatment allegations. As a result, racial factors are of little value in risk models.

**Misperception 3: Analytics is just a mathematical equation, not a comprehensive process.**

Analytics uses elements of statistics and mathematics, but the field of study is more than that. For child safety, analytics helps deliver a golden record of an individual, using accurate and complete data to find trends and patterns a human might miss. Once these cases are identified, it allows child advocates to be proactive. And analytics can encompass multiple scenarios (fatality, maltreatment, permanency, homelessness, education data such as attendance and test scores, etc.) to build a more complete picture of each case.

Collections of risk factors determine the level of risk, not individual facts or flags. This eliminates the one-size-fits-all approach to case response (e.g., children under age five are considered high risk and require a full investigation). Instead, a risk model can apply a score based on a number of factors to provide a more precise evaluation of each case. A high risk score means there is multitude of simultaneous risk factors present. The score—simply put—brings this to the attention of the case worker to help inform decisions, coupled with professional judgment.

**Misperception 4: Current, more static actuarial models are sufficient.**

One of the key benefits of analytics is that it can learn from the cases in the system and use a host of factors to determine the severity of each case. In fact, case workers themselves are a form of analytic models (biological, not mathematical). Unfortunately, they can't process more than a small set of data about the cases they are working.

So using the judgment of case workers—consensus decision making—will underperform more operational analytics due to:

- High case worker turnover rates
- Limited information available to the cases due to incorrect data (data quality issues) or overwhelming amounts of data
- High variations in case worker experience and judgment
- Case worker bias during the scoring process when using actuarial methods
- Case workers potentially manipulating the scores to force certain actions like removals

Operational analytical models work across the risk spectrum and can assist in screening and triaging cases based on available data. In addition, data can include information from a multitude of agencies to better inform the model and decisions, which allows for more accurate risk assessments in situations with limited report histories and offers a consistent summary of the typical risk observed for a child based on the data available to the agency.

In a recent white paper titled, "A Path Forward: Policy Options for Protecting Children from Child Abuse and Neglect Fatalities," released by the Commission to Eliminate Child Abuse and Neglect Fatalities, an initial finding was that "there is insufficient knowledge about the circumstances of child abuse and neglect fatalities and few proven strategies to prevent child abuse and neglect fatalities."[12] The report goes on to say, "Although thousands of children die because of abuse or neglect in the U.S. in a given year, unfortunately not much is known about the circumstances of these fatalities. Even less is known about which strategies have been proven to prevent child abuse and neglect fatalities. There is a clear need for a national research agenda on preventing child abuse and neglect fatalities. In addition, there are steps policymakers can take to maximize what we know from existing data."

The reality is that, as an industry, child protective services has continued to do things the same way for a long time and expect different outcomes. Innovation is a great catch phrase, but often moves at a snail's pace due to fear of change.

## IMPACT ON WORKFORCE

"What keeps you awake at night?" my colleague asked me. At the time, I was a child protective services administrator responsible for thousands of at-risk children on any given day. While there were many things that weighed on my mind, worker turnover created many sleepless nights, and days filled with anxiety and fear.

When I was an administrator, of all the things that impacted quality work, workforce stability was perhaps the biggest driver of quality outcomes. I would quickly see a direct correlation between workforce stability, case-load size, performance outcomes, financial performance, and client satisfaction. When worker retention was high, so was performance. When worker retention worsened, so did performance. Worker turnover was created by many things with a general understanding that turnover attributed to more turnover. Formal and informal stay and exit interviews provided some insight including:

- Too much paperwork
- Taking time off only added to work load upon return
- Not making enough impact
- Limited technology and tools needed to perform the job
- Fear of injury

High turnover and vacancy rates are not a recent phenomenon in the child welfare industry. However, the numbers above demonstrate that not enough has been done to truly address this issue. Most of what is accepted as sourcing, recruiting, and interviewing best practices today is largely based on conventional wisdom that is proving ineffective.

Very similar to how baseball evaluated potential and current talent prior to *Moneyball*, child welfare often takes a subjective and flawed approach to addressing workforce woes. These approaches are built on ideas that are convenient, appealing, and deeply assumed. It brings to mind a quote from Jim Pinkerton: "It's human nature to stick with traditional beliefs, even after they outlast any conceivable utility."

Common responses have included increases in salaries, decreases in minimum requirements (degrees and experience), more training, ineffective retention programs, and additional funding requests for more positions. We've seen the outcomes of these efforts.

In a recent presentation at a national child welfare conference, I asked an audience of more than 100 child welfare professionals how many of them were aware of a jurisdiction where more positions actually fixed a systematic problem such as turnover and opiate abuse. The response? You could have heard a pin drop. The reality is that many jurisdictions that do enjoy funding for new positions continue to struggle with turnover and high vacancy rates. I believe that is because they are not currently looking at the root of the problem, nor are they leaning on data to do so.

Workforce analytics can help build a better team! Child welfare can truly tackle this issue, much like professional sports and industry, but it will take much more than talking about reform and innovation. It will require action and disruptive innovation.

Workforce analytics can provide insights into issues such as recruitment processes (time to hire), and success factors, retention concerns, as well as overall workforce metrics. HR systems data on demographics, work history, recruitment, selection, payroll, promotions, behavior, and performance can be analyzed and surfaced through a visual dashboard that provides insights to better understand and solve the turnover issue.

If you can reduce unplanned turnover, cut the amount of time key positions are vacant, and improve your success in hiring the right candidates, you can make a dramatic difference in the ability to impact children and families.

In addition, it is better to utilize data to help inform recruitment, hiring, and retention practices by making usable data available to workers and leaders; this can have a tremendous impact on both worker retention and positive outcomes. Unfortunately, technology that has been put in place to make workers in child welfare more efficient and effective has actually done the opposite. Workers report that up to 55 to 60 percent of their time is spent doing administrative functions including data entry and reporting and less than 25 percent is spent on client-facing activities. While technology can help flip those numbers, I used to encounter a reluctance to embrace innovations that could impact the workforce and the children being served. As someone who has been in the trenches and led large child protective services operations, I truly believe in the power of analytics to support informed decision making that will help improve child welfare outcomes and save lives.

Technology now exists that can help surface needed information out of very large systems in a timely and usable way to help improve informed decision making while making workers more efficient and effective. Analytics is not just a trendy catch phrase, but a viable tool in the toolbox to help make child welfare prevent negative outcomes from occurring.

Implementing an operational analytic solution in a state and/or county child welfare system can actually impact worker efficiency and effectiveness by:

- Eliminating worker bias and the need for fidelity monitoring
- Decreasing time spent on administrative tasks and increasing the percentage of time on client-facing activities
- Helping workers prioritize case-related tasks
- Providing caseworkers with better information to help inform decision making on behalf of kids
- Allowing for an ongoing assessment of risk and safety based on real time or daily data feeds rather than at specific intervals throughout the life of a case (a lot can happen on a case between home visits)
- Helping inform inexperienced workers on risk levels and what factors attributed to risk to help inform placement and service related decisions
- Truly impacting the ability of a caseworker to have critical case-related information available at their fingertips

As previously stated, child welfare case workers are first responders and often engage families without much-needed information that can help ensure their safety and the safety of their clients.

In conclusion, preliminary findings of analytics in child welfare not only support, but demand that different approaches should be used to truly impact outcomes and save lives. Analytics is not the future of child welfare, but it is present if we truly want to improve childrens' well-being.

**Will Jones** is president and CEO of Thompson. Previously, he was a principal industry consultant for child well-being in state and local government practice at SAS Institute. He has over 21 years of progressive human services experience in diverse, mission-driven, nonprofit and government sector child welfare, juvenile justice, and behavioral health settings. He works closely with state and local agencies and leaders to solve problems and improve outcomes by using data analytics. He is a top-performing, executive-level operations professional credited with emphasizing innovation and creativity to solve complex problems via public and private partnerships in multiple states. He leads high-performing, cross-functional teams by inspiring data-driven, process-improvement initiatives that deliver results.

PROFILE

## NOTES

1. Paul W. Taylor, "Innovation May Be Scary, but Can Lead to New and Preferred Futures," *Government Technology Magazine* (September 2016), www.govtech.com/opinion/Innovation-May-Be-Scary-But-Can-Lead-to-New-and-Preferred-Futures.html.

2. Sarah Fass, Kinsey Alden Dinan, and Yumiko Aratani, "Child Poverty and Intergenerational Mobility," *National Center for Children in Poverty* (December 2009), www.nccp.org/publications/pdf/text_911.pdf.

3. Quinton Chandler, "Past Crime Rates Give Perspectives on Lower Juvenile Detention Numbers," *Alaska Public Media* (September 6, 2016), www.alaskapublic.org/2016/09/06/past-crime-rates-give-perspective-on-lower-juvenile-detention-numbers/.

4. 2014–2015 Santa Clara County Civil Grand Jury Report, "Child Abuse and Neglect Call Center, Can Every Call Be Answered?," https://assets.documentcloud.org/documents/3022191/Harvey-Rose.pdf.

5. Ibid.

6. Legislative Audit Division of Montana, "Review of Child Abuse and Neglect Investigations," (October 2015), http://leg.mt.gov/content/Publications/Audit/Report/14P-11.pdf.

7. Mark F. Testa, Michael W. Naylor, Paul Vincent, and Marci White, "Report of the Expert Panel: B.H. vs. Sheldon Consent Decree, " (July 21, 2015), www.aclu-il.org/wp-content/uploads/2015/07/BH-Expert-Panel-Report-Efiled.pdf.

8. 1News, "Shameful Child Abuse Record Prompts Protection for Officials Sharing Info about At-Risk Children," *1News Now* (August 17, 2016), www.tvnz.co.nz/one-news/new-zealand/shameful-child-abuse-record-prompts-protection-officials-sharing-info-risk-children.

9. Naomi Schaefer Riley, "How Big Data Can Help Save Endangered Kids," *New York Post*, October 16, 2016, http://nypost.com/2016/10/16/how-big-data-can-help-save-endangered-kids/.

10. Claudia Melendez Salinas and James Herrera, "State Report: Child Protective Services Must Change Intake Practices," *Monterey Herald* (February 24, 2016), www .montereyherald.com/article/NF/20160224/NEWS/160229864.

11. Ibid.

12. Commissioner Cassie Statuto Bevan, Hope Cooper, and Marci Roth, "A Path Forward: Policy Options for Protecting Children from Child Abuse and Neglect Fatalities—Draft," (November 24, 2015), https://www.acf.hhs.gov/cb/resource/ cecanf-final-report.

# CHAPTER 3

# Education

*Nadja Young*

# INTRODUCTION

*Education, then, beyond all other divides of human origin, is a great equalizer of conditions of men—the balance wheel of the social machinery.*[1]

—Horace Mann

Julie was born to two teenage parents, in a trailer, in rural South Carolina. Winters brought her parents the tough decision of paying for food or heat. They opted for food and set up blanket tents in the trailer for Julie and her brother to sleep beneath to generate body heat. Throughout elementary and middle school, Julie's teachers regularly documented concerns in her permanent file about how her home life was impacting her schooling.

Nadja was raised by a single mother who was on and off government assistance in Virginia. Nadja's father spent 15 years in federal prison. Her mother had stints in mental health institutions and county jail at different times in her childhood. Social services temporarily removed Nadja from her home after 35 days of being absent or tardy in the fourth grade.

Early data paints a picture of two girls with the odds stacked against them who probably should have been low achieving. Low income, check. Parents without college degrees, check. Chronic absenteeism, check. One fatherless home with crime and mental illness, double check. Both girls had parents who loved them, but who were ill-prepared and ill-equipped to provide the life structure needed for academic success. Yet, both girls went on to graduate from college, earn graduate degrees, and become public school teachers themselves. Julie went so far as to earn a Doctorate in Mathematics Education.

The teachers in their South Carolina and Virginia schools did not allow out-of-school data factors to label Julie and Nadja and serve as excuses for low performance. These girls were not written off. Instead, strong teachers and principals used in-school performance data to see

Julie and Nadja's potential. They used data for good to insist upon academic excellence that provided a stairway out of the circumstances in which they were born. Education changed Julie and Nadja's lives and was the great equalizer proclaimed by Horace Mann in 1848. I am a product of the great equalizer. I am Nadja.

Unfortunately, for too many children, schools are not able to fulfill this promise. While Julie and I were able to beat the odds, our siblings did not fare as well. Julie's parents learned that her younger brother was two grade levels behind in reading in the third grade. My mother found out when my little sister was in middle school that she was three grade levels behind in math. Many parents in America don't know what they don't know about education. They rely on experts in schools to manage their children's learning and alert them if something is wrong. Inconsistencies in educational experiences, like the ones Julie's and my family experienced, are inexcusable because children's life opportunities are hampered as a result.

If our nation's schools cannot address these inconsistencies, they will potentially leave millions of kids behind. Julie's and my family stories are not just useful anecdotes. 17.4 million children live in fatherless homes.[2] 16 million children live in poverty.[3] 1.7 million children have a parent in prison.[4] Our stories resemble big data on millions of real children in America. So how can we use big data to begin to address the issue?

There is a myriad of data points swirling around each student—from demographics and poverty indicators, to prior course grades and test scores, to attendance, discipline, behavioral, and physical health needs. While the basic information about a student is readily available, how students learn best and are likely to perform in the future is trickier to tabulate.

Educators believe in their hearts that all students can learn. But I have also seen educators allow out-of-school data factors to serve as excuses for underachievement or to influence perceptions about students, thereby limiting rigor and opportunity. National achievement data shows that our public education systems work well for students with means. And not so well for already disadvantaged students. Racial achievement gaps are found in the National Assessment of Education Progress (NAEP), also known as the "Nation's Report Card." On the 2015 NAEP Mathematics eighth-grade assessment, black students scored 32 points lower, on average, than white students.[5] More alarming, the achievement gap between children from high- and low-income families is widening. It was roughly 30 to 40 percent larger among children born in 2001 than among those born in 1976.[6] The socioeconomic status of a child's parents has always been one of the strongest predictors of the child's academic achievement and educational attainment. This was true for Julie's little brother and my little sister. But it doesn't have to be this way. Julie and I also lived on the poverty line, yet our schools managed to help us reach the highest academic levels. Public school systems must accomplish this for all students.

When research shows that poor students tend to be lower achieving, conventional wisdom could prompt policymakers to focus on solving the poverty problem to improve academic outcomes. However, poverty is a larger, and perhaps impossible, problem to tackle in a four-year political term or average 3.2-year tenure of a chief state school officer.[7] In the meantime, state leaders can strive for better performance measurement, find schools that are beating the odds, and use the strength of the evidence to guide expansion of the best programs, practices, and policies.

States should strive for better performance measurement when looking at the contradictions in public education statistics. In 2014–2015, the U.S. high school graduation rate rose to an all-time high of 83.2 percent,[8] yet various sources cite an average of 40 percent of college freshman are not "college ready." A 2011 report by the National Governor's Association states that "approximately 40 percent of all students and 61 percent of students who begin in community colleges enroll in a remedial education course at a cost to states of $1 billion a year."[9] In these cases, students are paying full tuition for noncredit-bearing coursework—courses like Algebra I that they passed in high school in order to get a diploma but didn't master.

While state test proficiency rates generally increased under No Child Left Behind (NCLB) accountability systems, this was in part due to many states lowering the proficiency bar, or cut scores. In contrast, 2016 NAEP results showed a drop in twelfth graders' math scores and no improvement in reading—results unfortunately consistent with those previously released for fourth and eighth graders.

For an international mismatch, U.S. state standardized test scores rose under NCLB while our nation slipped on international benchmark tests such as The Programme for International Student Assessment (PISA). Out of 34 countries administering PISA in 2012, the U.S. ranked 27th in math, 17th in reading, and 20th in science.[10] This reflects a drop from our nation's ranking amongst 32 countries in 2000: 18th in math, 15th in reading, 14th in science.[11]

These contradictions provide a gut check. U.S. educators and policymakers need to get honest about student performance through better measurement. State leaders who think they already have measurement systems and data dashboards in place should to take a second look. It's not just about providing more big data but equipping our schools and teachers with data that can make a difference. In order to use education *data for good*, decisions must be first based on *good data*. Performance metrics that are more fair, accurate, and stable require some pretty sophisticated analytics.

Why bother investing time and money to move beyond test scores and spreadsheets to use analytics? Because, to borrow from Maya Angelou, when educators know better, they can do better. When teachers know more about their students' needs and their own strengths and weaknesses, they can teach more effectively. I spent seven years as a career and technical education teacher in two states. The 1,200-plus students I taught deserved the best possible educational opportunities. So do my two daughters in public schools today. Students in all communities deserve the best possible education experience public schools can provide.

Teachers need better information to drive instructional improvement. Administrators need better information to drive school improvement. Policymakers need better information to drive program investments and accountability systems. The many data points that tell the stories of children and schools need to be boiled down to actionable insights in order to be useful. Just like a car dashboard provides critical information about the health of a vehicle, education data provides critical information about the health of our school systems and their ability to serve all student groups. A car dashboard provides warnings and indicators when something is wrong. Auto mechanics gather further diagnostic information from in-car computers to fully understand problems and fix them. Likewise, education data provides signals about achievement gaps and underperformance, but educators and policymakers then need diagnostic information to determine how to fix the problems. Like automotive engineering, improving our nation's schools depends much on data, mathematics, and analytics.

If a teacher were about to embark on a cross-country field trip with a group of students, she would want the most reliable car and navigational tools. I spent my early years in the classroom feeling uncomfortable with data and uncertain about how to use it for the benefit of my students. I was driving cross-country each academic year without any predictive information or navigational tools. I had to navigate with intuition and wait for a breakdown to know if anything was wrong. I've now dedicated my post-teaching career to ensuring that educators are armed with better information to drive students toward their full academic potential and that policymakers have analytic tools to drive smart, evidence-based, policies and wise investments of taxpayer dollars.

Let's explore how states can navigate this education analytics journey.

## BUILD YOUR ENGINE—BUILD THE EDUCATION DATA SYSTEM INFRASTRUCTURE

Before a car can be driven, it must have a well-built engine and frame. Before education data can be analyzed, it must first be collected, cleansed of errors, linked, merged, and stored. Building the data infrastructure as a foundation for education analytics is imperative. Equally important is that these systems are built at the state level so that data can follow each child in a standardized manner as they move across schools and districts in a state.

Nearly every state has made significant investments building State-wide Longitudinal Education Data Systems, often called SLEDS, SLDS, P–16, P–20, or P–W (workforce) systems. In 2005, the Data Quality Campaign identified 10 essential elements of statewide longitudinal data systems and began measuring states' progress toward implementing them. The 10 essential elements provided a transparent comparison of states as they built systems to collect, store, and use longitudinal data to improve student achievement. States had a long way to go in 2005 and this public comparison provided an important first incentive to make progress.

Federal incentives then followed. Since 2005, the U.S. Department of Education has awarded grants worth $265 million to 41 states and the District of Columbia.[12] In 2007, the federal *America COMPETES Act* codified 12 "Required Elements of a P–16 Education Data System," which include DQC's 10 essential elements. In 2009, the federal *American Recovery & Reinvestment Act* required states, as a condition of receiving state fiscal stabilization funds, to commit to building data systems consisting of these 12 elements.

1. A unique identifier for every student that does not permit a student to be individually identified.
2. The school enrollment history, demographic characteristics, and program participation record of every student.
3. Information on when a student enrolls, transfers, drops out, or graduates from a school.
4. Students' scores on tests required by the Elementary and Secondary Education Act (now the Every Student Succeeds Act).
5. Information on students who are not tested, by grade and subject.
6. Students' scores on tests measuring whether they're ready for college.
7. A way to identify teachers and to match teachers to their students.
8. Information from students' transcripts, specifically courses taken and grades earned.
9. Data on students' success in college, including whether they enrolled in remedial courses.
10. Data on whether K–12 students are prepared to succeed in college.
11. A system of auditing data for quality, validity, and reliability.
12. The ability to share data from preschool through postsecondary education data systems.

Getting all 12 elements in place was no small task for states. To understand the magnitude, Connecticut has just over 550,000 students, but the state's SLDS contains over 150 million rows of data. North Carolina's P20-W contains over 50 tables, 892 data elements, and 92,517 unique values. Florida's SLDS cost over $14 million to build over three grants and 10 years, plus ongoing maintenance.[13] By 2011, most states had the majority of the DQC's 10 essential elements in place. In 2014, the final year of DQC's survey, three states had implemented all of them: Arkansas, Delaware, and Kentucky.[14]

Building these SLDSs was a big first step for states to collect and store education data in a standardized way. However, very few educators or policymakers have *access* to the data sitting in their SLDS. Imagine these data warehouses as huge locker rooms with a locker for each child in a state. But few administrators at the state level have the keys to the locks, and it is time consuming to find the right locker when someone needs to pull out their contents. Running a query can take days or even weeks to pull the data files and get answers to questions. Just because a state has built an SLDS does not mean that student data is being put to work to help teachers and students. These data then have to be analyzed to transform them into insights that are useful to a teacher, administrator, or policymaker. Once analyzed, these insights need to be reported in a way that educators and policymakers can consume. Now that states have made such huge strides in building these SLDS engines, policymakers and educators need analytics to use the data for good, to drive sound policy decisions, and ultimately improve student outcomes.

## USE THE DASHBOARD TO MEASURE WHAT MATTERS MOST—STUDENT LEARNING GROWTH

Good drivers frequently look at their car's dashboard to monitor speed, fuel levels, and RPMs in order to make quick course corrections. Sometimes warning lights indicate something needs attention, such as tire pressure or oil levels. It is evident which alerts are most critical and demand immediate attention, such as the "check engine" light (see Figure 3.1).

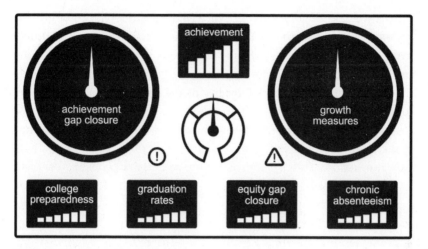

**Figure 3.1** Dashboard Gauges

In education, there are endless debates about what types of academic and nonacademic metrics are important for accountability systems. These accountability systems are what prompt schools to make changes and course corrections to move the needle on different performance indicators. Access to rigorous coursework and the arts, reductions in absenteeism and discipline referrals, standardized test scores, and graduation rates—all are important to create well-rounded school environments. Many are of interest to parents trying to select a school for their children. But if I had to boil it all down to one lever on the dashboard that I would want to obsess over, I'd put a stake in the ground on student growth. As a parent and former teacher, academic growth, or improvement, is what matters most to me. It is at the heart of why I devoted myself to the profession and how I chose the particular public school for my daughters. Research also shows that high student growth is correlated to future economic success and improved quality of life.[15] So let's explore the student growth topic.

### How is growth different from achievement?

Achievement measures provide a snapshot of what a student knows at a single point in time in a given grade and subject. Achievement is often defined by the test score a student earned on one day, under a specific set of conditions.

Growth, on the other hand, refers to the amount of student learning (or lack thereof) that took place over time. For a simple example, what was a student's average achievement level at the start of the year, and at the end? And what's the difference between the two?

A focus on growth acknowledges that, academically, students don't all start the year at the same place. Not all students can become high achieving—or even proficient—by the end of the year. But regardless of their achievement level, all students can grow. At the very least, they can maintain their achievement level relative to their peers and not fall further behind.

## Why is growth a more fair measure of school quality?

Every state's system for evaluating academic success focuses on achievement in some part, as required by the *Every Student Succeeds Act.*[16] But achievement is only one part of the picture—and one that can be affected by many influences, such as demographics, socioeconomics, and other student characteristics. Students' achievement levels are typically most highly related to economic status.[17] This means that students from high-income families tend to be higher achieving. Students from low-income families tend to be lower achieving. And these factors are out of educators' control.

For example, the scatterplot in Figure 3.2 illustrates publicly available data from Tennessee showing average achievement on the state

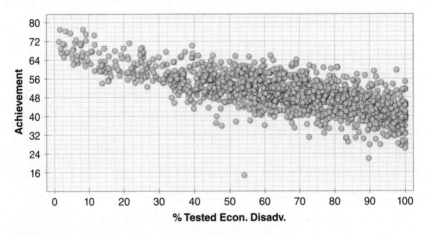

**Figure 3.2** Math Achievement across Grades 4–8 in 2015
*Source: Tennessee Value-Added Assessment System (https://tvaas.sas.com).*

math assessment in 2015 across grades 4–8. Each dot represents an elementary or middle school across the state. Schools are sorted on the x-axis by the percentage of students considered economically disadvantaged by qualifying for free or reduced price lunch. There is a strong trend showing that average achievement levels decline with household income levels.

On the contrary, learning *growth* typically has little to no relationship with a student's background. Empirical evidence from public growth data in Tennessee shows that students can make low, average, or high growth at all ends of the socioeconomic spectrum (see Figure 3.3). Instead, growth is highly dependent on what happens as a result of schooling. By including a sound measure of growth in accountability systems, policymakers put the emphasis on something educators can influence.

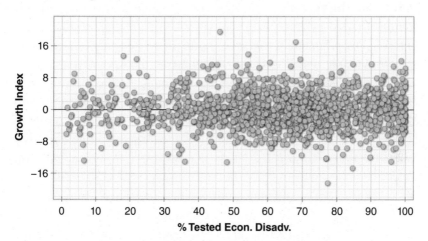

**Figure 3.3** Math Growth across Grades 4–8 in 2015
*Source: Tennessee Value-Added Assessment System (https://tvaas.sas.com).*

Advancements in technology and computing power allow Tennessee's big data to be crunched more quickly and accurately each year so that educators can use this information in an interactive way to bust myths, diminish human bias, and revolutionize new approaches to teaching and learning.

Educators can't control which students walk through their school house doors or classroom doors. They can't control how far behind students might be on day one of school based on disabilities, being new to the English language, being poor, hungry, or moving around a lot. Likewise, they can't control how advanced students might be because they have two married college-educated parents, went to a stellar summer camp, or have a library of enriching books at home. Educators have to meet students where they are, at the start of each school year or semester, and craft the most individualized learning plans to help take each student farther. Teachers and schools can control how much learning, or academic growth, takes place within the time they have a student in their class or school, making growth a more fair measure of school quality for accountability purposes.

**Why is growth hard to measure?**

When tracking schooling effectiveness over time, simply using changes in test scores or proficiency rates can be problematic for a variety of reasons. Year over year test score changes in given grade (such as fourth-grade reading scores in 2015 versus 2016) actually reflect achievement for different cohorts of students. Tracking one cohort across grades is difficult when statewide assessments change over time (South Carolina and Ohio, for example, have had three different state tests in three years). Proficiency benchmarks and cut scores are moving targets that can also change over time. Additionally, most states have a mix of assessments that includes statewide assessments and locally adopted or created tests at the district level, as well as Advanced Placement (AP) and college readiness tests, such as the ACT and SAT. These assessments are all on different scales and their scores are not comparable. To make matters worse, students move around or miss tests, creating holes in their testing history. Lastly, there is measurement error, or noise, around each individual test score that must be accounted for. A student may have a good test day, or a bad test day. Each test score is merely an estimate of what a student knows on a given day—and may not cover all the student has learned—or hasn't learned—about the subject. All this said, test scores are imperfect. If states want to incorporate growth measures in accountability systems, then simple growth measures will not adequately compensate for these testing challenges.

One way to minimize and account for the challenges with testing, or achievement, data is through analytics. An advanced growth or value-added model can use all available testing data (even as tests change over time), include more students (even if they have missing data), and provide results in more grades and subjects.

Advanced growth or value-added models can analyze the longitudinal data sitting in an SLDS to transform test scores into more fair, accurate, and stable measures of student progress. This new reflective and diagnostic information can then be used to better understand the strengths and weaknesses in our education systems, schools, and programs.

As states assemble the various indicators of school system health on their dashboard, it's important that they include better student growth data along with the many other real time data elements. Because when educators know how they've done in the past, they can make better-informed decisions for the future.

## USE THE NAVIGATION SYSTEM TO GUIDE EDUCATION POLICY

While the data dashboard is critical to maintain the school system's health, the education driver also needs a strong navigation system, powered by evidence, to decide when to change lanes and make adjustments for improved student outcomes. State leaders should consider what formal or informal policies are in place to incent educators to use student data for good. At the end of the day, teachers, counselors, and principals are busy. District and state administrators are busy. Educators are overwhelmed with their current workloads and may not take the time to investigate student data, interpret it, and explore necessary changes. Education policies can provide the levers or guardrails to increase the use of analytic insights for the improvement of schools, programs, and student learning. The following initiatives are in play in some fashion in nearly every state:

1. Accountability Systems and School Report Cards

    The 2015 *Every Student Succeeds Act*[18] requires states to measure and report on the performance of eight student groups on academic indicators such as test scores, graduation rates, achievement gap closure, and English-language proficiency. The proposed federal regulations stipulate that an optional academic indicator "measure either student growth or another valid and reliable statewide academic indicator that allows for meaningful differentiation in school performance."

The eight student groups include: low-income students, students of color, students with disabilities, English learners, migrant, homeless, foster, and military-connected children. Including student growth measures in state accountability systems and school report cards gives a clearer picture of how well schools are meeting the needs of smaller, and potentially more vulnerable, student groups that could otherwise get lost in the aggregate.

2. Evaluating Interventions and Program Effectiveness

I regularly attend House and Senate Education Committee meetings across our 50 states. Inevitably, someone comes to the podium asking for more state money to be invested in a specific program such as a reading program, math program, mentorship program, pre-kindergarten program, year-round schools, smaller class sizes, instructional coaches, ed-tech tools, and so on. But those testifying seldom bring the data to say, "Students who participated in this particular program grew more than expected, and here's the evidence." Legislators and taxpayers alike want to see the evidence of impact, or proof that an investment will pay dividends in student learning before appropriating more money year after year. Even when our nation increases education spending, some complain that we don't see the results because if we are only looking at test scores as evidence of impact, that moving target can be elusive as standards and testing rigor keep increasing. Could student learning growth be the answer? One Pennsylvania school district thinks so.

A small school district outside Pittsburgh has earned numerous accolades, with each school in the district winning the U.S. Department of Education's coveted Blue Ribbon award. Yet there was one group of students the district wanted to better serve: those with learning disabilities. By using a value-added growth model, the district was able to better track year-to-year growth for all students, see which interventions worked, and which needed retooling. Administrators discovered that one group of low-achieving students benefited from a course that was more closely aligned with the core curriculum than its standard literacy intervention program meant for struggling learners. By eliminating a program that didn't provide a return on their investment, the district was able to save money and better serve struggling students. In 10 years, the passing rates have jumped from 14 percent in math and 29 percent in reading to 69 percent for both subjects.[19] While this story illustrates just one school district's findings, imagine the potential cost savings and bump in student learning if all of America's 13,500-plus school districts used evidence to drive decision making in the same way.

3. Equity Plans[20]

In 2014, the U.S. Department of Education (USED) began the Excellent Educators for All initiative, "designed to move America toward the day when every student in every public school is taught by excellent educators."[21] The initiative was further strengthened by being included in the Every Student Succeeds Act (ESSA) with bi-partisan support. As part of the initiative, each state education agency (SEA) is required to submit to the USED a state equity plan to ensure equitable access to excellent educators that ensures "poor and minority children are not taught at higher rates than other children by inexperienced, unqualified, or out-of-field teachers." One chief requirement that state equity plans have to meet is to identify equity gaps in poor and minority students' access to "highly effective," "effective," or "ineffective" teachers.

Compelling research indicates that teacher quality is the single most important school variable affecting student achievement.[22] "The more impoverished and racially isolated the school, the greater the likelihood the students will be taught by inexperienced teachers, uncertified teachers, and out-of-field teachers who do not hold a degree in the subject they are assigned to teach. Schools with these characteristics are invariably low-performing schools."[23] Kati Haycock, founding director of the Education Trust, maintains that about half of the achievement gap would disappear "if we only took the simple step of assuring that poor and minority children had highly qualified teachers."[24] She continues to argue that, "Even though some states and communities have made efforts to correct the inequitable distribution of high-quality teachers, none have committed themselves to an all-out effort to assure that poor children are taught by teachers of at least the same quality as other children. We need—as a nation, as states, as communities, as institutions and as individuals—to do just that."[25]

This state equity plan requirement begs the question: Are states adequately differentiating teacher effectiveness to even begin identifying these equity gaps? In the 2009 study, *The Widget Effect*, TNTP (The New Teacher Project) found that "less than 1% of teachers received unsatisfactory ratings."[26] If teacher evaluation systems rely too heavily on subjective observation rubrics, principals end up rating the majority of teachers effective or highly effective, making them all look about the same in quality like widgets. Furthermore, the Bill & Melinda Gates Foundation's Measures of Effective Teaching (MET) project found that observation ratings alone were not very predictive of a teacher's future success at helping students learn.[27] MET researchers asserted that value-added analysis, which uses test results to gauge how much an individual teacher contributes to his or her students' learning growth, is more accurate than any other single measure in predicting success over the course of a teacher's career—more than classroom observations or student surveys. Connecting value-added measures to individual teachers is one of the best ways to adequately differentiate teaching effectiveness for the purpose of identifying equity gaps. But to do this at the local level alone is nearly impossible.

States have tens of thousands of teachers at a given time, with thousands entering and leaving the workforce annually. Within each school year, students move in and out of classrooms, schools, districts, and states. I once taught a freshman who had attended 35 different schools by the ninth grade. Accurately tracking equitable access to effective teachers for all students is a big data problem that requires a state-level analytics solution.

Tennessee's equity plan is one state model to consider as it uses teacher, subject, and grade level growth measures to differentiate teacher effectiveness into five levels and investigate the following key equity questions:

- Do Tennessee students have equitable access to highly effective teachers?

- What factors affect students' access to highly effective teachers?

- What is the current supply of highly effective teachers in Tennessee?

- How are highly effective teachers distributed within districts and schools in Tennessee?

- What are we doing and what can we do to improve students' access to highly effective teachers?

Data from Tennessee shows that, on average, students who score at the lowest proficiency level see the largest gains after having a highly effective teacher for two or more consecutive years. Yet, low-performing students are less likely than their higher-performing peers to have access to the best teachers. Tennessee's *Equitable Access to Excellent Educators* report shows that in 2014–2015, in grades 4–8 math classes, "only 45 percent of the lowest performing students had a highly effective teacher while 55 percent of advanced students had a highly effective teacher. To improve student achievement for all students, Tennessee is working to ensuring that all students have access to effective teachers and that lowest-performing students are not systemically assigned to lower-performing teachers."[28]

For a strong local example of how school districts can act upon state equity plans, Guilford County Schools in North Carolina serves as a model.[29] After using value-added reporting for more than a decade, the school system has a longitudinal, data-driven means to measure teacher effectiveness that has propelled significant increases in student achievement while also reducing teacher turnover. This 72,000-student school system noticed that its best teachers were clustered in higher socioeconomic schools. In order to improve reading and math scores for third through eighth grades and passing rates for high schoolers, Guilford County wanted to draw highly effective teachers to schools with a higher percent of low-income students. Rather than offer bonuses to any teacher to work in low income schools, Guilford first identified teachers with high value-added growth results and then recruited them to Mission Possible schools where they earned bonuses of up to $12,000 a year for increasing student performance above district averages.

The results of the Mission Possible program were dramatic. "We've been able to show significant increases in the percentage of students who are passing the elementary reading, math and high school subject tests in 97 percent of our program schools," explains Dr. Amy Holcombe, Executive Director of Talent Development. "We've had increases of 47 percent in some schools for certain courses. We've also decreased teacher attrition from 36 percent to as low as 10.7 percent."

Like Tennessee and Guilford County Schools, no state or district can reduce equity gaps until they first identify where those gaps exist and then devise precise strategies to improve upon the situation. When education leaders know better, they can do better. Honest measurement about teacher effectiveness through advanced growth or value-added modeling is the first step to identifying and shrinking equity gaps for disadvantaged students.

4. Educator Evaluation

In 2015, 43 states required teacher evaluations to include measures of student growth.[30] Twenty-three states used evaluation systems to make teacher tenure decisions. Sixteen states used evaluation systems for performance pay initiatives. As state policymakers choose to include student outcomes data in evaluation systems, they must do so in the most responsible and legally defensible way possible. Decades of research have confirmed that teachers are the most important in-school factor for improving student achievement, or academic growth.[31] Leading education researchers such as Sanders, Goldhaber, Hanushek, Chetty, Friedman, Rockoff and others, have spent the last three decades analyzing big data on teacher quality and its impact on student learning. To sum it all up, their findings show that teachers are game changers and have significant impact on education policy today.

- **Teaching matters.** The differences in teaching effectiveness have a highly significant effect on the rate of student academic progress.[32] These effects are most pronounced in math.

- **Teaching matters a lot because ineffective teaching cannot be compensated for in future years.**[33] Teacher effects are found to be cumulative and additive. In other words, if a student has two very ineffective teachers in a row for the same subject, then there is very little evidence that a subsequent teacher can make up that loss in progress. Furthermore, the sequence of teachers that a student has (and whether those teachers are effective or ineffective) greatly affects the possibility of that student passing a high-stakes test.[34]

- **Most of the differences in the rates of student progress can be attributed to classrooms rather than schools or districts.** About 65 percent of student growth is attributable to teacher quality, 30 percent to school quality, and 5 percent to district quality.[35] This reinforces the importance of teachers on their students' academic opportunities.

- **A teacher's effectiveness is primarily related to the teacher, rather than the school environment.**[36] When teachers change schools, their effectiveness persists, or follows them to their new school. Teaching effectiveness ratings do not change to mirror the effectiveness of the new school, even when teachers move to schools that are very different in socioeconomic status from their original school.

- **Effective teachers don't just improve test scores, they improve life outcomes for students.** A 23-year Harvard and Columbia University study published in 2011 shed new light on the long-term impacts of teachers with both high and low value-added estimates. Researchers tracked math and reading assessment data on over 2.5 million students from 1989 to 2009. They then incorporated 90 percent of these students' tax records from 1996–2010 to analyze the long-term outcomes. They found the return on investment for students placed with a single, high value-added teacher included: higher college attendance, increased lifetime earnings and retirement savings, residence in better neighborhoods, and reduced odds of teenage birth.[37]

Evidence indicates that teachers with high growth and value-added measures help students in school and life. That is difficult to refute. Even if those growth measures are not a formal part of a teacher's evaluation by factoring into a final effectiveness rating, it is important to measure and show teachers their student impact data for their own reflection and improvement purposes. Diagnostic information extends from these analytic models to illuminate teachers' strengths and weaknesses in growing different types of learners.

Michelle Watts is a middle school English language arts and reading teacher in Texas' Lubbock Independent School District. She acknowledges the new insights she gains from this diagnostic data: "It's very important to me to know how I'm doing as a teacher every year. When we get our (student growth) results it allows me to see the students I'm most successful with. And some years I'm right in my guessing. But two years ago I was completely blown away with the data that I saw because I thought I was more highly effective at motivating low-achieving students. But actually, I was better at growing my middle and high-achieving groups of students. So, to me, (growth data) doesn't change what I teach, it changes my focus in what I teach, and that's the difference."

These diagnostic data can then be used to guide principal–teacher coaching discussions and teachers' individual growth plans to lift the mass of teachers that fall in the middle of the bell curve with average effectiveness. This is the starting point to targeted professional development and elevating the teaching workforce at large.

5. Educator Preparation Improvement

Once states begin generating teacher-level growth data, a next extension is to also use that student impact data to inform and improve Educator Preparation Programs (EPPs). The colleges, universities, and alternative certification programs that prepare our nation's teachers already collect a myriad of data for accreditation and federal reporting requirements. EPPs have vast input data about their completers (such as their SAT/ACT scores, high school and higher education GPAs, course and clinical hour completion, etc.). But they often lack outcome data for each completer—specifically, data on the growth of the K–12 students that their graduates are teaching. Stakeholders need a way to complete the feedback loop between K–12 and higher education by connecting the state's extensive data on student outcomes with the data that EPPs have on their graduates in order to:

▪ Understand which EPPs stand out in preparing the most effective teachers in specific program areas. Tennessee's *Report Card on the Effectiveness of Teacher Training Programs* shows that teachers from Lipscomb University, Memphis Teacher Residency, and Teach for America Nashville consistently produce teachers who are more highly effective than the average novice and veteran teachers across the state.[38] Shouldn't every policymaker know which EPPs are the star performers in their state? And once they know, what good could be done with that information?

▪ Understand why some EPPs are more effective than others at producing highly effective K–12 teachers by linking student growth data to other EPP program and completer data. These additional metrics could include: endorsement area, degree type, mentorships, clinical versus credit hours, transfer status, K–12 school placement, and traditional academic markers like GPA, SAT/ACT, and certification test scores. These linkages may point to relationships between programmatic elements and student learning outcomes that can drive educator preparation policy changes.

■ Use insights to improve how EPPs prepare teachers by scaling up what's working. States can analyze all of this data at once and visualize results to inform EPPs about best practices within and across institutions. For example, if having a higher ACT or SAT score is not related to greater teaching effectiveness, then states do not necessarily need to prioritize raising entrance requirements into EPPs as related to those standardized tests. But, what if that relationship exists for math teachers only? Then perhaps the entrance requirements could be more targeted for specific program areas and degree types. Or if a state finds that the effectiveness of a mentor teacher has a strong relationship with a student teacher's effectiveness in their first three years of teaching, then this new insight could be used to set policy about who can be a mentor teacher.

Teachers and administrators are often awash in information, but rarely have reliable clarity about their students or their own performance. Analytics boil down what seems like far too much data to ferret out important insights that educators might otherwise miss and produce useable guidance. Instead of all the coordinates on a map, analytics provide the navigation system voice that says "turn left and go straight for 4.7 miles."

## LOOK THROUGH THE WINDSHIELD WITH PREDICTIVE ANALYTICS

So far this chapter has highlighted how important reflective data can be to educators and policymakers. It's important to note that analytics can take that same historic data sitting in an SLDS, and turn it into predictive information as well. While the rearview mirror, dashboards, and navigation systems are imperative to safe driving, so too is the windshield to look at the road ahead. Predictive analytics can make education decisions easier so teachers can clearly see a path through their windshields and hit the gas on the first day of school trusting they are going in the right direction.

With all of the data collected about students' past performance, there is no reason why it should take teachers two, four, or six weeks at the beginning of each school year to spot struggling learners, and those ready for enrichment. A middle school principal should know exactly which entering sixth graders are at risk of failing the end-of-grade reading or math tests so that they can be supported by the right programs over the summer or at the start of the school year, before they flounder. A high school principal should know which current ninth graders are likely to score a 3 or 4 on AP tests so that they can be placed in appropriate pre-AP course sequences to keep them on that path to success. And if schools truly want to deliver on the promise of delivering personalized learning, it can be more quickly realized with predictive analytics.

All of a students' prior testing history holds the information needed to produce projections to future academic milestones like future state tests, PSAT, SAT, ACT, AP exams, and college readiness. But it does require advanced analytics to transform many different test data points into future projection data. Once done, this can eliminate the guesswork for teachers, counselors, principals, parents, and students alike.

Student projections can be used at the beginning of the school year to support students' unique needs more proactively. This is already done in states such as Tennessee, Ohio, and Pennsylvania where the U.S. Department of Education has found their projections to be more accurate three years in advance of a test, than using an immediate prior year test score as a predictor.[39] Educators should consider how student projections and predictive analytics could be used systematically to support:

1. Response to Intervention (RTI)—a tiered process used to systematically identify students' academic and behavioral needs, intervene, and track the responses to interventions at different levels of magnitude.[40]
2. Early warning indicators for students at-risk of failure or dropping out.
3. Increasing access to enrichment and more rigorous coursework.
4. Differentiated instruction and lesson plans.
5. Student course placement decisions based on likelihood of success.

6. Matching teachers and students more strategically for best fit.

7. Personalized learning environments where students work on individualized content.

Policymakers should consider how student projections and predictive analytics can help with the following legislative initiatives:

1. Early Literacy Policies

According to a 2014 Education Commission of the States (ECS) report, 16 states plus DC require the retention of third-grade students who do not meet grade-level expectations in reading.[41] Twenty-five states plus DC administer early reading assessments statewide in grades K–3. Predictive analytics can use those K–3 reading assessments to project a student's likelihood of reaching proficiency on each state's third grade reading assessment. Thus enabling educators to provide the right interventions to prevent student retention in the third grade.

2. Advanced Coursework Policies

as of May 2016:[42]

■ Eight states and DC require all high schools or districts to offer Advanced Placement (AP) coursework.

■ 20 states offer a financial incentive to support AP course offerings.

■ 29 states offer AP fee reductions or waivers to low-income students.

■ 30 states include AP participation and/or performance measures in district or high school accountability reports.

Increased AP access and financial supports are great first steps to help more students earn college credit while in high school. The uptick in accountability ties should stimulate enrollment. A remaining concern is whether the increased enrollment will be equitable, or if poor students and students of color will be disproportionately underenrolled. Predictive analytics and student projections to AP success can tell educators and policymakers how many students are strong candidates for this more rigorous coursework so that they can meet the demand with adequate teaching staff and curricular resources. Parents should also have access to their children's projections so that they can be better informed advocates during their children's course scheduling and parent–teacher conferences.

Principals at Union Middle and Union High School, both small, rural schools in North Carolina, challenged themselves to increase enrollment in AP courses (English, calculus, and U.S. History) especially for first-generation college students. The feeder schools vertically aligned and used predictive analytics in middle school to ensure optimal course placement for their students in the ninth grade to provide a well-connected path to success. Working with the AVID (Advancement Via Individual Determination) program allowed for team building and content alignment. Then came the crucial question: Now that we have built it, will they come? Enrollment in AP courses more than doubled. All students in the first cohort of first-generation college students graduated and were accepted into college. Multiple students earned scholarships, including two full rides to prestigious North Carolina Universities. Dr. Theresa Melenas, AVID Director and Principal at Union Middle School, noted, "The use of projections helped us to open doors for many of our students who had never considered college. As early as middle school, we are able to provide enrichment and support to continue to challenge students academically. As these students transitioned to high school, we were better prepared to support them as they enrolled in more challenging courses."

3. College Readiness Projections and Parent Reporting

Just as students and parents should have access to AP projections, they should also be looking ahead to college readiness and which postsecondary institutions are likely options. In North Carolina and Tennessee, if a student dreams of being an engineer, for example, she could know in middle school if she is likely to score high enough on the SAT or ACT, respectively, in order to graduate successfully from engineering degree programs in specific in-state universities. If she finds she is not on the right trajectory, she still has four high school years to take more rigorous coursework to better prepare for that ACT or SAT and improve her chances of reaching her postsecondary goals. Furthermore, if a projection shows that a student is likely going to need to take a remedial class in college, why not tell the student as a freshman, so they can try to beat that projection by mastering the material in high school? By successfully completing remedial coursework while still in high school, students would save valuable money and time. Julie's and my parents didn't have a clue about what we needed to be prepared for college or to get accepted into college. Julie and I had to figure it out on our own with the help of friends, teachers, and counselors. Schools need to engage and enable parents with this type of information and pull them into these discussions earlier. Better data can promote more productive college planning discussions.

4. Math Placement Policies

Taking algebra in eighth grade is considered a key stepping stone that allows students to progress to calculus by twelfth grade. Students who take calculus in high school have a greater chance of successfully finishing a four-year college degree—particularly if they want to major in a STEM (science, technology, engineering, or math) field. As a result, students can have a broader range of life choices. Decades of research back this up. Early access to algebra has a sustained positive effect on students leading to more exposure to advanced mathematics curriculum and, in turn, higher mathematics performance by the end of high school.[43] Taking advanced math courses in high school is more strongly associated with successful completion of college than any other factor including high school grade point average and socioeconomic status.[44]

Most everyone agrees on the importance of algebra. But deciding when to place students in Algebra I has been a hotly contested issue in states. Predictive analytics and student projections can help place students in the course when they are ready and most likely to be successful. North Carolina's largest school district has recently successfully implemented this policy. The Wake County Public School System has nearly tripled enrollment in eighth-grade algebra while maintaining proficiency rates above 95 percent.[45] Successful initiatives like this usually start small. In this case, it was led by a visionary principal in one Wake County middle school.

Before using projections to help select algebra students, Wake Forest Rolesville Middle School (WFRMS)[46] did what the majority of schools still do—relied on teacher recommendations. Teachers routinely weeded out any pre-algebra students they didn't think could handle algebra. What the WFRMS math teachers discovered is that many of the students not recommended for advanced math were doing very well on class tests—but they were getting average to poor grades for other reasons, such as not turning in homework.

To test the algebra projections, former Principal Elaine Hanzer first encouraged teachers to put all the pre-algebra students who had a high probability of succeeding into algebra. Then she recruited one teacher to teach a class of students who hadn't taken pre-algebra, but were recommended through the analytics. The teacher offered extra help to catch the students up. At the end of the first year, every student recommended by analytic projections passed the statewide algebra test.

In order to make this culture shift a success, Hanzer's team met extensively with students, parents, and teachers to explain the program and the reasons for placing students in algebra. Meanwhile, administrators began laying the groundwork to get more students into advanced sixth grade math and pre-algebra in seventh grade.

In the second year, the projections identified nearly half of all eighth graders had at least a 70 percent chance of reaching proficiency at a school where slightly more than 50 percent of the students are considered economically disadvantaged. The passing rate that year was 97 percent.

Hanzer says there has been a culture change at WFRMS that turns conventional education wisdom on its head. Maintaining a class notebook, turning in homework, class participation, organization, neatness, and projects are deemphasized in grading and course placement recommendations. Teachers can no longer dock students for putting their name in the wrong corner of a paper, "or not folding it a certain way," says Hanzer, who found these grading practices disproportionately affected poorer students who have less support at home. Instead, as she learned with the algebra placements, challenging students and telling them they can handle advanced subject matter has a positive impact on work habits. "Those habits changed as the second semester rolled in," Hanzer says. "It's harsh to say, but teachers have prejudices. (Projection data) takes prejudices out and you start dealing with fact; you know what a student is capable of."

The windshield of this education vehicle allows educators to look into the future to avoid likely accidents and hazards, to avoid lengthy detours, and take the smoothest path toward student success. If policymakers and administrators have the data sitting in their states to produce predictive insights, why doesn't every state invest in analytics to improve opportunities for students? And for states that already have these types of predictive reporting, why do not all educators use it? As Principal Hanzer experienced, building a data culture in schools is hard. It take courageous leadership to trust data, train people, and stick with it long enough to see if the results play out in students' favor. Courageous leaders need to drive the car.

## DRIVE THE CAR AND USE THE DATA

The best car in the world is useless if it just sits on the lot. The best data and analytics, unused, can't change practice. People, processes, and culture do. Teachers, administrators, and policymakers alike need to drive these cars to get students safely through this cross country field trip that is K–12, and graduate them ready to take on the world of work. Although culture shifts are difficult, we must start somewhere. Using sound data is an effective way to take emotions and anecdotes out of conversations and bridge gaps to focus on what's best for kids.

Some educators are apprehensive about investing time in data. They see data as facts and figures. But it's more than that. It's the lifeblood of our schools. It contains history. And it can tell us something about the future. In order for educators to drive with student data, it must be easy to use. No one wants to drive an unreliable clunker. Education data must be delivered through reporting that is accessible, intuitive, interactive, and secure. Security is critical as data privacy continues to be a concern for parents and the public. Role-based permissions for sensitive student and teacher data help to ensure that the right adults view the right students' information. Yet at the same time, transparency is important for appropriate school and district-level information to be shared publicly with policymakers, parents, and researchers. Training and professional development around data literacy is also needed so educators feel supported and empowered to use data reporting for good, rather than see it as a foregone conclusion.

Policymakers want to reward success by using data as a flashlight, not a hammer. They want to ensure each and every tax dollar is being used in a program that positively impacts citizens, and most importantly, children. And they want to be certain that they're investing money in outcomes—not just spending money on a legacy program that's been around forever, or a shiny, new system that's never been tested. In order to do this, they need evidence. Education scholar Chester Finn wrote in his 1986 book *What Works*, "It is not reasonable to expect research to resolve all issues or to erase all differences of opinion. We can but supply some information that we think reliable, and we will continue in the future to supply more. But it is up to the American people to decide what to do. The better their information, the wiser will be their decisions."[47]

Analytics provide this type of reliable information, or good data, to make our teachers and leaders wiser so that they can use data for good. They can then identify what's working, fix what isn't, and discover new opportunities for students. Big data is really just a bunch of small stories, which together have huge impact. There are millions of American students like Julie and me whose data stories might not initially look so rosy. Teachers have to know kids to grow kids. Analytics help teachers know kids faster and better. Analytics cut through the big data noise and illuminate student potential so that educators can be game changers for all of our children.

**PROFILE**

**Nadja Young** is a Senior Manager of Education Consulting at SAS Institute. She is a former teacher, certified by the National Board of Professional Teaching Standards, with an M.Ed. in secondary education. Young bridges gaps between analysts, practitioners, and policymakers to help state and local education agencies better use data to improve student outcomes. Prior to joining SAS, she was a career and technical education teacher and wrote statewide project management curriculum and assessments for the North Carolina Department of Public Instruction.

## NOTES

1. L. A. Cremin, "The Transformation of the School: Progressivism in American Education, 1876–1957" (New York: Alfred A. Knopf, 1961).

2. "Living Arrangements of Children under 18 Years and Marital Status of Parents, by Age, Sex, Race and Hispanic Origin and Selected Characteristics of this Child for All Children: 2014," Washington, DC: U.S. Census Bureau, www.census.gov/hhes/ families/data/cps2014C.html.

3. Jason M. Breslow, "By the Numbers: Childhood Poverty in the U.S.," Public Broadcasting System (2012), www.pbs.org/wgbh/frontline/article/by-the-numbers -childhood-poverty-in-the-u-s/.

4. Lauren E. Glaze and Laura M. Maruschak, *Parents in Prison and Their Minor Children* (U.S. Department of Justice, Bureau of Justice Statistics, August 2008), www.bjs .gov/content/pub/pdf/pptmc.pdf.

5. G. Bohrnstedt, S. Kitmitto, B. Ogut, D. Sherman, and D. Chan, *School Composition and the Black–White Achievement Gap* (Washington, DC: U.S. Department of Educa- tion, National Center for Education Statistics, 2015), https://nces.ed.gov/pubsearch/ pubsinfo.asp?pubid=2015018.

6. Sean F. Reardon, "The Widening Academic Achievement Gap Between the Rich and the Poor: New Evidence and Possible Explanations" (Stanford University/Russell Sage Foundation, 2011), https://cepa.stanford.edu/sites/default/files/reardon%20 whither%20opportunity%20-%20chapter%205.pdf.

7. Andrew Uijfusa, "Turnover, Growing Job Duties Complicate State Chiefs' Roles," *Education Week* (January 2015), www.edweek.org/ew/articles/2015/01/28/turnover -growingjob-duties-complicate-state-chiefs.html.

8. Alyson Klein, "Graduation Rate Hits Record High of 83.2 Percent: Should Obama Take Credit?" *Education Week* (October 2016), http://blogs.edweek.org/edweek/ campaign-k-12/2016/10/graduation_rates_hit_another_h.html.

9. Ryan Reyna, "Common College Completion Metrics," National Governors Association (2010), www.nga.org/files/live/sites/NGA/files/pdf/1007COMMON COLLEGEMETRICS.PDF.

10. Andreas Schleicher and Michael Davidson, "Programme for International Stu- dent Assessment (PISA) Results from PISA 2012" (Paris, France: Organisation of

Economic Co-operation and Development, 2012), https://www.oecd.org/pisa/keyfindings/PISA-2012-results-US.pdf.

11. M. Lemke, C. Calsyn, L. Lippman, L. Jocelyn, D. Kastberg, Y. Liu, S. Roey, T. Williams, T. Kruger, and G. Bairu, "Outcomes of Learning: Results from the 2000 Program for International Student Assessment of 15 Year Olds in Reading, Mathematics, and Science Literacy" (Washington, DC: U.S. Department of Education, National Center for Education Statistics, 2002), http://nces.ed.gov/pubs2002/2002116.pdf.

12. U.S. Department of Education, "Statewide Longitudinal Data Systems," (2009), www2.ed.gov/programs/slds/factsheet.html.

13. National Center for Education Statistics, "Statewide Longitudinal Data Systems Grant Program," https://nces.ed.gov/programs/slds/state.asp?stateabbr=FL.

14. Data Quality Campaign, "10 Essential Elements of Statewide Longitudinal Data Systems" (2014), http://dataqualitycampaign.org/why-education-data/state-progress/.

15. Raj Chetty, John N. Friedman, and Jonah E. Rockoff, "The Long-Term Impacts of Teachers: Teacher Value-Added and Student Outcomes in Adulthood," National Bureau of Economic Research, 2011, www.nber.org/papers/w17699.pdf.

16. GovTrack, "S. 1177—114th Congress: Every Student Succeeds Act," (October 6, 2016), www.govtrack.us/congress/bills/114/s1177.

17. James S. Coleman, Ernest Q. Campbell, Carol J. Hobson, James McPartland, Alexander M. Mood, Frederic D. Weinfeld, and Robert L. York, "Equality of Educational Opportunity" (Washington, DC: National Center for Educational Statistics, 1966), files.eric.ed.gov/fulltext/ED012275.pdf.

18. See U.S. Department of Education, Every Student Succeeds Act (ESSA) online resource at www.ed.gov/essa?src=rn.

19. SAS, Inc., "Expanding Growth Opportunities for All Students," www.sas.com/en_us/customers/fox-chapel-area-school-district.html.

20. State equity plans and federal requirements can be viewed at the U.S. Department of Education's website at www2.ed.gov/programs/titleiparta/resources.html.

21. United States Secretary of Education, "Letter of November 10, 2014 to Chief State School Officers," www2.ed.gov/programs/titleiparta/equitable/letter11102014.html.

22. Cynthia D. Prince, "The Challenge of Attracting Good Teachers and Principals to Struggling Schools," *American Educator*, January 2002, www.aft.org/periodical/american-educator/winter-2002/attracting-well-qualified-teachers-struggling.

23. Ibid.

24. Kati Haycock, "Good Teaching Matters. How Well-Qualified Teachers Can Close the Gap." *Thinking K–16* 3, no. 2 (Summer 1998), edtrust.org/wp-content/uploads/2013/10/k16_summer98.pdf.

25. Ibid.

26. Daniel Weisberg, Susan Sexton, Jennifer Mulhern, and David Keeling, "The Widget Effect. Our National Failure to Acknowledge and Act on Differences in Teacher Effectiveness," Second Edition, The New Teacher Project, www.widgeteffect.org.

27. The Bill and Melinda Gates Foundation, "Gathering Feedback for Teaching: Combining High-Quality Observations with Student Surveys and Achievement Gains" (2012), http://k12education.gatesfoundation.org/teacher-supports/teacher-development/measuring-effective-teaching/met-feedback-for-better-teaching-nine-principles-for-using-measures-of-effective-teaching/.

28. "Tennessee Department of Education, "Equitable Access to Excellent Educators" (2015). www2.ed.gov/programs/titleiparta/equitable/tnequityplan9115.pdf.

29. SAS, Inc. "Improving Teacher Effectiveness." www.sas.com/en_us/customers/guilford-county-schools.html.

30. NCTQ State Teacher Policy Yearbook 2015. "Executive Summary" (2015). www.nctq.org/dmsView/2015_State_Policy_Yearbook_Executive_Summary.

31. W. L. Sanders, and J. C. Rivers, "Cumulative and Residual Effects of Teachers on Future Student Academic Achievement (Research Progress Report)" (Knoxville, TN: University of Tennessee Value-Added Research and Assessment Center, 1996), www.cgp.upenn.edu/pdf/Sanders_Rivers-TVASS_teacher%20effects.pdf.

32. R. A. McLean and W. L. Sanders, "Objective Component of Teacher Evaluation: A Feasibility Study," Working Paper No. 199 (Knoxville, University of Tennessee, College of Business Administration, 1984).

33. Sanders and Rivers, "Cumulative and Residual Effects."

34. June C. Rivers, "The Impact of Teacher Effect on Student Math Competency Achievement." Unpublished doctoral dissertation, University of Tennessee Knoxville (1999).

35. SAS Inc. internal research.

36. W. L. Sanders, S. P. Wright, and W. E. Langevin, "The Performance of Highly Effective Teachers in Different School Environments," In Matthew G. Springer (ed.), *Performance Incentives: Their Growing Impact on American K-12 Education* (Washington, DC: Brookings Institution, 2009).

37. Raj Chetty, John N. Friedman, and Jonah E. Rockoff, "The Long-Term Impacts of Teachers: Teacher Value-Added and Student Outcomes in Adulthood," Columbia Business School (2011), www.rajchetty.com/chettyfiles/value_added.htm.

38. "Tennessee Teacher Preparation Report Card 2014 State Profile," https://www.tn.gov/assets/entities/thec/attachments/reportcard2014A_Tennessee_State_Profile.pdf.

39. "Ohio Growth Model Application and Information." U.S. Department of Education (August 19, 2008), www2.ed.gov/admins/lead/account/growthmodel/oh/index.html.

40. Rachel Brown-Chidsey and Mark W. Steege, "Response to Intervention: Principles and Strategy for Effective Practice," 2nd ed. (New York: Guilford Press, 2010).

41. Emily Workman, "Third-Grade Reading Policies," Education Commission of the States (December 2014). www.ecs.org/clearinghouse/01/16/44/11644.pdf.

42. Education Commission of the States, "50-State Comparison: Advanced Placement Policies," www.ecs.org/advanced-placement-policies/.

43. Julia B. Smith, "Does an Extra Year Make Any Difference? The Impact of Early Access to Algebra on Long-Term Gains in Mathematics Attainment," *Educational Evaluation and Policy Analysis* 18 (Summer 1996):141–153.

44. Clifford Adelman, "Answers in the Tool Box: Academic Intensity, Attendance Patterns and Bachelor's Degree Attainment," Washington, DC: U.S. Department of Education, Office of Educational Research (1999), www.ed.gov/pubs/Toolbox.

45. Wake County Public School System, "WCPSS Pushes to Enroll Qualified Students in Algebra," Wake County Public School System Blog, August 30, 2011, webarchive.wcpss.net/blog/2011/08/wcpss-pushes-to-enroll-qualified-students-in-algebra-i/.

46. SAS, Inc., "Expanding Eighth-Grade Algebra Participation," www.sas.com/en_us/customers/wake-forest-rolesville.html.

47. Chester Finn, Jr., "Introduction: What Works: Research About Teaching and Learning," U.S. Department of Education (1986), http://files.eric.ed.gov/fulltext/ED263299.pdf.

# CHAPTER 4

# Healthcare

*Jeremy Racine*

was the firstborn to a single mother of what would soon be three children by 1979. We lived well below the poverty level and my mother relied on vital government social services for our family upbringing. When it came to healthcare, we were members of the Medicaid health program and also received assistance from nutrition programs such as WIC and SNAP. While we did receive access to vaccines, primary/specialized care, and food, it was far from perfect. Nutrition in particular was a severe challenge. There was little guidance from our providers or nutrition programs to help support typical nutritional needs and we established what would become long-term habits which, I believe, led in part to my own costly chronic conditions (GERD and peptic ulcers). While it took me 30-plus years to change my own habits, I can't help but think of how technology, namely data and analytics, might have provided a more preventative course of action. It could have provided insight to my providers on my comprehensive medical history, nutrition, and other variables, in addition to a better understanding of how others have responded to treatment options. This level of technological maturity simply didn't exist yet and our healthcare system was designed as a volume-based system that incentivizes based on the volume instead of the value of care. In an age where widespread digitization within the healthcare ecosystem is our current reality, data and analytics can play a positive disruptive role, accelerating innovation within the healthcare decision-making process and leading to better access to high-quality care within a system moving toward care value, not volume.

## ROLE OF THE GOVERNMENT

The government has clearly matured into a monumental role player in today's healthcare ecosystem. They are truly involved in nearly every aspect of healthcare, from policymaking to funding opportunities to administering many government-run health programs (Medicare, Medicaid, CHIP, state employee health plans to name a few) to operating a variety of agencies such as the Centers for Medicare and Medicaid Services (CMS), the Centers for Disease Control (CDC), and the Office of the National Coordinator for Health Information Technology (ONC). As we think of the role of the government and its ability to leverage, as well as support and promote data and analytics, consider the Zika virus

## Zika Virus

The Zika virus has been identified as a potential biological threat to the United States. The government plays a vital role in the prevalence, prevention, and treatment of the disease through policy, funding, programs, and care delivery. The ability for a virus like Zika to become an epidemic is real, but in many cases it can be significantly contained by the use of data and analytics by the government. Following is a small list of government agencies. Data from these agencies could be shared and analyzed. This would allow the data to be significantly more beneficial and may provide valuable insights, especially when information is needed quickly to address an outbreak like Zika where time is of the essence.

- **Centers for Disease Control:** The Epidemic Information Exchange stores and disseminates information around most recent disease news, consultations among peers, outbreak reporting and more to public health professionals, including state and local public health organizations.
- **Customs and Border Patrol:** Maintain information about entries into the United States, including prescreening information.
- **Environmental Protection Agency:** Maintain data on mosquito control programs that when analyzed on their own could provide information on effectiveness of the program, factors which may help or hurt programs, and forecasting capacity to execute on more programs.
- **State and Local Data Sources:** Health Information Exchanges (HIEs) contain clinical electronic medical record data on patients from across the state and can be analyzed by both state public officials and service providers to understand emerging clinical indicators, strategic interventions, effectiveness of treatment programs, and interactions with other comorbidities (other conditions/diseases). Hospital discharge data also provides much of the same basic information as above, but it is not nearly as

comprehensive. States with All-Payer Claims Databases will also have another set of data—claims data meant for health insurance claims billing. This data has a number of clinical identifiers and can be used in conjunction with HIEs to supplement data and potentially fill in gaps where HIE data may be missing or incomplete.

- **Country data, World Health Organization, United Nations:** While Zika may be an emerging threat and data is not as prevalent (as of 2016), data from other mosquito-borne illnesses is valuable. For instance, since the same species of mosquito carries Dengue fever, historical data from Dengue fever would enable a starting point to becoming more analytical with data that would be expected to be somewhat similar to Zika and at the very least could be used to look at mosquito transmission, prevalence, and prevention efforts.[1] Zika data from these other countries may be available as well as historical and current data on other mosquito-borne illness. Analytics can be used to identify trends in disease prevalence, effectiveness of prevention/treatment programs, mosquito programs and their success, social determinants, financial impact, and also forecast these trends.

Clearly the data from each of these organizations can be analyzed and used for their own significant purpose. However, if all of this data from each organization was brought together and analyzed, the relationship they share could have a compelling effect. For example: Let's say the CDC acts as a central point for all this data; we will call it the CDC Analytics Center of Excellence, a central area to aggregate data from various sources with the goal of holistically analyzing the collective data and disseminating analytic results to all participating organizations as well as federal, state, and local government officials. The CDC could use analytics to mine this information store, which now would consist of all of the data from each of the organizations listed above, and look at historical trends and root/cause analysis for disease prevalence, the impact of weather, social determinants (such as economic status, race, gender), travel, education, as well as clinical/claim data from providers and facilities that indicate the effectiveness of treatments as well as prevention efforts and best practice sharing methods. For example:

Zika prevalence is rapidly increasing in the southern regions of Florida and the state of Florida has been in contact with the CDC for assistance in responding. The CDC Analytics Center Of Excellence would be able to assist Florida with a rapid response including:

- Understanding and predicting future growth patterns based on current Florida demographics, but also risk adjusted based on data it now has from other countries or regions of the United States that have dealt with similar Zika or other mosquito-borne diseases.

- Already have access to Florida's clinical, claim, and hospital discharge data and be able to analyze and predict clinical indicators, prevalence, and outcomes as well as trends about transmission. Additionally, it could also share which clinical interventions were most successful in other areas of the country/world and help Florida make better decisions about overall strategic clinical responses, including resources, treatments, programs, education, and funding.

- Share mosquito-control data and analysis on which programs were most effective and might be most effective from similar climates/terrain and help Florida to enhance its decision-making process for additional funding and/or future policy around mosquito control. Additionally, since the CDC has clinical data on outcomes and treatments, analytics could be shared that may indicate potential side health impacts from certain programs.

- Provide analysis on entry points into the United States as well as successful screening programs to help Florida predict which interventions, if any, would be most effective and preventative at points of entry into the state.

- Analyze the data it receives from Florida to help Florida improve its response efforts in addition to improving efforts across the nation and sharing its data/analytics with world organizations for improvements across the globe.

It is important to walk through such an example as it may not be readily apparent how much the government currently does, and potentially could do, to enhance its response for containment of a deadly virus like Zika. Clearly, the government plays a very significant role and relies on constantly evolving data/analytics innovation for decision support. Zika is just one example of the many health issues our country faces and it is essential that the government ensure its policy and programs are aligned with the realities and mature technological needs of today's healthcare environment, and that our providers, facilities, and patients across the United States are ready for today and whatever is next. The government's efforts are vital to continue our innovative progress toward enhancing delivery of care and to improve health outcomes for you and the entire population.

 **EXTRACT**

The integration of primary care and public health is ultimately about the daily bidirectional exchange of health information needed to improve people's lives. For example, automated case reporting from an electronic medical record to a public health agency can vastly improve timeliness, completeness, and accuracy of population health measurements allowing the analytics to directly save lives in the event of a public health emergency, or reduce morbidity through predictions that are actionable for a community.

Jeffrey Engel, MD, executive director, Council of State and Territorial Epidemiologists, former state health director and state epidemiologist for North Carolina.

## THE CHALLENGE

As U.S. healthcare costs continue to rise to almost unimaginable levels, our health outcomes, as measured by life expectancy, have failed to rise in comparison to many developed nations. Figure 4.1 illustrates this disturbing trend:

While U.S. spending has gone from under $500 per capita in 1970 (6.9 percent GDP) to almost $10,000 per capita (17.5 percent GDP) in 2014, life expectancy in the same time frame has gone from 70.8 in 1970 to 78.8 in 2014.[2,3] Comparatively speaking, the countries of Israel, Spain, South Korea, and Chile all have life expectancies over

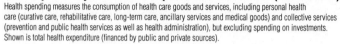

## Life expectancy vs. health expenditure over time (1970-2014)

Health spending measures the consumption of health care goods and services, including personal health care (curative care, rehabilitative care, long-term care, ancillary services and medical goods) and collective services (prevention and public health services as well as health administration), but excluding spending on investments. Shown is total health expenditure (financed by public and private sources).

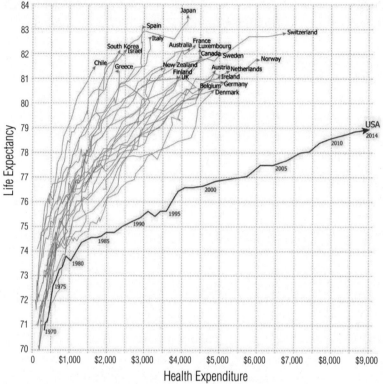

Data source: Health expenditure from the OECD; Life expectancy from the World Bank. Licensed under CC-BY-SA by the author Max Roser. The interactive data visualization is available at OurWorldinData.org. There you find the raw data and More visualizations on this topic.

**Figure 4.1** Life Expectancy versus Health Expenditure
*Source: https://www.equities.com/news/life-expectancy-in-the-us-is-flatling-while -healthcare-costs-go-up.*

80 with spending at or below approximately $3,000 per capita (a fraction of the U.S. spend); and, more astonishingly, these countries accomplished this almost 20 years ago! With U.S. national healthcare costs expected to exceed $5 trillion (20 percent GDP) by 2025 we might presume that with such funding we should enjoy the luxury of a globally superior health system that produces the highest-quality

healthcare and the resultant substantial increase in life expectancy, but this simply isn't the case.[4] While the United States does enjoy some of the most innovative and modern healthcare services in the world, it struggles to narrow the gap in quality care and outcomes between economic classes. In fact recent studies have found the "gap in life expectancy between the richest 1 percent and poorest 1 percent of individuals was 14.6 years (95 percent CI, 14.4 to 14.8 years) for men and 10.1 years (95 percent CI, 9.9 to 10.3 years) for women."[5] With such a large gap in health between classes it is fair to presume that the delivery of and access to quality healthcare in the United States is not as guaranteed or consistent as we might think. The system has been challenged for many years; think about some very basic questions when it comes to care.

- How is quality of care defined or measured? (Is it an outcome, such as range of motion within a time frame following knee surgery, or government-driven guidelines/metrics, peer reviews, word of mouth, advertisements/marketing?)
- How much will this cost? (What are the out-of-pocket costs short and long term, and how do they compare to other service providers and facilities with similar metrics?)
- Are all my care providers communicating and collaborating?
- What is the government doing to help with the questions above for the entire healthcare system (healthcare programs, policies, funding, standards, technology)? Can they do more?

Pose these same questions when it comes to various other purchases, such as a house, car, or which restaurant to enjoy a meal at, and the resources for making a more informed decision are seemingly endless. Shouldn't we expect the same for healthcare? There is no decision in any one person's life that should be more important than a decision related to health. After all, without your health, how would you even be in a position to make other decisions? Decisions involving healthcare are almost never simple and have profound, life-changing effects—from the provider and patient working on treatment, to payers trying to better manage their programs, to pharmaceutical companies trying to create cutting-edge drugs, to the government and the many roles it plays in healthcare—and we should all be engaged in ways in which these decisions can be better supported.

What if there were more robust data and analytics that could be used to make more informed decisions about what affects us the most, and be applied to the decision-making process for those in the government who create policy and programs, for government programs that administer our public health and social services, for the payers that insure us, the providers that treat us, the pharma companies that create life-changing drugs, and for the people? The data is here, and it needs to be more transparent, put to better use, and enhanced with advanced analytics encouraged by the government, innovated by the private sector, and leveraged by all. While there are many opportunities for improvement, let us walk through three areas where data and analytic initiatives can make a compelling impact.

## Population Health

When I think of population health, I think not just health but health and everything that impacts health. Consider this: studies suggest that healthcare on its own is only responsible for 10 percent of all premature deaths in the United States; compare this to 40 percent for behavioral patterns, 30 percent for genetic predisposition, 15 percent for social circumstances, and 5 percent for environmental exposure.[6] What is clear is the predominant factor in premature deaths actually has little to do with only healthcare; collectively it covers just about every other aspect of life. What is fair to say is that to truly understand the health of any population is an exercise that can be tremendously enhanced if knowledge of everything that shares an impact with health is considered. What is learned at a population level can also be applied at an individual level, so what we create is a cyclical approach to population health focused on gathering as much health/nonhealth data about a person, then aggregate it collectively to analyze trends on different population groups, and again learn from these trends and apply back at the individual level—a cycle of learning and improving. Think of everyday life and the many variables that impact our health—genetics, where we live, the jobs we perform, people we interact with, food we

**Figure 4.2** The Variety of Data that Impacts a Population's Health

eat, places we go, education we receive, social services we receive, financial decisions we make, and so many more (see Figure 4.2).

Additionally, our health also impacts most, if not all, of these nonhealth-related social actions. For many of these health and social activities (called determinants) we have devices, applications, or other means of collecting data about the associated event, program, activity, or place. As an example, I have MyFitness Pal, Nike Run Club, Road Bike Pro, credit card/banking/investment data online, education/travel/taxes/job/social service data online, and, of course, my electronic medical data.

How much data is being generated? EMC estimates that health care data will reach 2,314 exabytes by 2020.[7] Let me paint a picture: if we took just 295 exabytes (a fraction of the 2,314), writing all that data to older CD-ROMs (539 MB compressed data per CD) would equal about 404 billion CD-ROMs, and based on an approximate thickness of 1.2 mm per CD if you were to pile up all those CD-ROMs it would make a stack from the earth and extend into the sky and well beyond the moon, for big data that's a data supernova![8] So where is most of this data coming from?

The private sector continues to push the edge of innovation in the health data market. In the mobile world alone, an IMS Institute for Healthcare Informatics research report notes that in 2015 there were 165,000 different health and medical applications available.[9] The same study finds that most of these apps are basically of little relevance, with 12 percent of the 165,000 apps being attributed to 90 percent of all health and medical app downloads. Meanwhile, in the electronic medical record space, according to healthit.gov, "As of July 2016, 632 vendors supply certified health IT to 337,432 ambulatory primary care physicians, medical and surgical specialists, podiatrists, optometrists, dentists, and chiropractors participating in the Medicare EHR Incentive Program."[10]

Clearly there are massive amounts of data and many choices of technology, so the question then seems obvious: What do we do with all this data?

There are many places for the use of all this data. The Zika example we previously discussed is one of those, but population health is not just analyzing things at a population level; it depends on and clearly impacts at the personal level—the two are highly intertwined.

Let's first look at things through the eyes of a person and start with my own example. As I mentioned in the beginning of this chapter I suffer from chronic digestive issues. I had a pretty complex and stressful year in 2014, and a very challenging one for managing my own health. I was going through a recent divorce in the beginning of the year, traveling extensively for work, preparing a house to sell, and made some less than ideal financial investments among my everyday challenges. I worked with my providers as my health changed through the year, but for the most part my provider was acutely focused on how I was feeling that visit instead of the historical and future management of a chronic condition. By the end of the year I switched to a new primary care provider who was part of an ACO (Accountable Care Organization) and subscribed to holistically treating the patient. They also participate in a Health Information Exchange. After reviewing my history and discussing nearly every impactful health/nonhealth data point including my travel patterns, divorce, eating, exercise, financial stresses and more, we were able to start to create a path to better management of my condition. I can't help thinking that there were obvious enhancements that could have helped me and my provider be more preventative and strategic.

- Ideally, all the online and device data I had should easily be sent to my provider or to a Health Information hub. That wasn't possible and still is not the case today (2017). We had to spend time reviewing the data manually, one group of data at a time, with little analytics or additional technology to assist in the decision-making process.

- What if I had a solution that could integrate all of the data I choose to include and utilize this holistic data locally for myself as well as submit it to an HIE, my provider, and others?

- What if this solution could use analytics to also compare my medical condition and contributing factors (maintaining anonymity) against other people who have similar medical conditions?

- What did their treatment look like? How successful was it (both in quality of life and cost)?

- Were there education or awareness campaigns that might be helpful for me?

- Wouldn't my data also be helpful not just to me, but also to public health officials and others who want to track the prevalence of disease, strategic interventions and their effectiveness from a cost and quality perspective, understand contributing factors regionally or by other population demographics (race, age, gender, etc.)?

This is where data, analytics, and the cyclic approach can provide tremendous value within a population-health initiative. Employing analytics on the collective data that stretches across my historical health/nonhealth activity is initially helpful to me and my provider and could be used to be more preventative and more precise with my treatment. As we learn more about myself and the outcomes of my treatment we could share results via national, state, and local databases such as HIEs or other similar health data hubs. Here, all my data would be housed, creating a comprehensive view of myself and the rest of the population who submit data. Since this hub has data from a variety of patients similar to me, analytics such as trends, forecasts, risk scoring, and other predictive elements could be calculated and disseminated to assist the provider community in their decision-making process and lead to higher-quality, more effective outcomes. This cycle of learning and improving continues as I see my provider on future visits, data from the rest of the population may have been analyzed and analytics provided indicating changes to my treatment that might be more beneficial to my health. The same population data could be analyzed and health/nonhealth factors could be considered for future new or amended government policies and programs, and for biosurveillance initiatives to manage biological events such as the Zika example.

This kind of innovative approach to using data and analytics to help answer these questions and improve care also requires tighter public and private sector collaboration and support to ensure that:

- Innovative best practices are (to the extent possible) discussed, shared, and applications/data interfacing is considered between public and private health IT initiatives, such as HIE's, All-Payer Claims Databases, and Medicaid Enterprise Systems.
- National/State HIT Projects such as HIEs and APCDs, which exist in many states across the country, look to analytics not only to assist the government in better understanding the health of their population and improving upon it, but also demonstrate and provide value to the many entities (such as health insurance payers, providers, facilities, and researchers) who currently are or in the future will provide funding for such projects.
- National, state, and local efforts continue to innovate applications and infrastructure that can collect and analyze healthcare clinical and claims data in addition to other data, such as wearable devices (insulin pumps, pacemakers, etc.).
- Data can be more easily leveraged and analyzed. This is especially important as we are currently struggling to successfully

create state and national databases with clinical (EMR), claim (insurance), and social determinant data that provide the needed value.

To summarize, making the best use of all this data to better support clinical decision making ideally needs the following:

- Access to and the technological means to collect all my personal data (that I authorize).
- Technology to match all my data together and ensure there is a single, consolidated view.
- A place to securely store all collected data, a massive information hub that maintains anonymity and is only identifiable by name to me, my provider(s), or for national emergencies.

Analytics that analyzes all this data to:

- Provide analytically driven clinical decision support at the point of care based on predictive analytics (also called precision-based medicine; think of using all the device data discussed in addition to the EMR and other sources to support providers decisions).
- Analyze and identify strategic interventions and programs for addressing specific chronic conditions, such as diabetes, hypertension, and cancer (using data/analytics to better understand what works, what isn't working, and how we can optimize treatment and outreach to provide education and allocate funding to address chronic conditions in populations).
- Analyze the costs and clinical effectiveness of healthcare programs and policies.
- Analyze the impactful relationships among healthcare and non-healthcare data (residual costs associated with recidivism, incarceration, education, productivity, welfare). For example, would enhanced funding for early intervention programs yield long-term gains such as lower crime rates, reduced strain on social services, and increased worker productivity from a particular population?

- Engage with patients and improve the patient experience. What are the best ways to engage with patients, especially given the many ways in which technology can be used? Which outreach campaigns are most effective and why?

- Enhance coordination of care and integration efforts that allow service providers and all stakeholders to have rapid access to a single source of data to analyze and coordinate treatment options in a collaborative environment.

- Better understand the social impacts of healthcare utilization (for example, how is healthcare access, quality, and cost different for those with stable housing and food versus those without?)

While there are certainly many questions to ask and areas to improve, the future is bright. The government is in a unique position, they have the ability and the potential governance to ingest data from electronic medical records and insurance claims data in addition to the many social-determinant data they already house. By uploading wearable device data, genomic data, and other determinant data they could enable one to receive more precise care through the dissemination of this data and the application of analytics that considers nearly every contributing factor to healthcare.

Examples of successful population health-related initiatives are everywhere. They are rampant in the private sector where funding is driven primarily by revenue but they are gaining momentum in the public space as well.

The San Bernardino County Department of Behavioral Health understands the vital role that data and analytics plays in population health initiatives. The department collects data from a variety of disparate data sources to form a more holistic view of the residents it serves. While the primary data sources are behavioral health in nature, the department realizes the impactful relationship that other data like physical health, criminal justice, and other social services contain and has included these data and their owners in its analytic endeavors. As San Bernardino's analytic initiatives have continued to mature and innovate, the department now relies on analytics to guide its operations—everything from service strategy and community outreach to improving the quality of care. Through their efforts they have helped reduce hospital readmissions, improve health outcomes, enhance decision making across the organization, and even reduce stigma, an often overlooked area of population health.

## ▶ EXTRACT

Data analytics is essential to truly understanding the health of our population and telling the story of our consumers and services. The deep connections between health and nonhealth data have very real meaning and potentially profound effects on the lives of our residents. Utilizing analytics enables our partners and us to better serve our residents by more effectively advocating for stigma reduction and needed care and promoting awareness, wellness, resilience, and recovery in our community.

Dr. Joshua Morgan, Chief of Behavioral Health Informatics,
San Bernardino County Department of Behavioral Health.

The government has made great strides in population health analytics with continued commitment to data-analytics innovation through many of its own agencies and programs. However, recent studies have indicated that the cycle of population health relies heavily on the states to invest in innovation. Specifically a Northeastern University study states "environments they encounter are also shaped by the extent to which state governments are adopting and promoting population health objectives by benchmarking health improvements through metrics like the County Health Rankings, establishing State Health Improvement Plans, or participating in the Centers for Medicare and Medicaid Services (CMS), State Innovation Model Initiative (SIM), or the Delivery System Reform Incentive Program, both of which have population health improvement components."[11] Clearly the government and private sector need to continue to work closely with each other and maintain their mutual commitment toward innovation with data and analytics to continue to provide the opportunity for enhancements to population and personal health outcomes. In closing on this topic, my colleague at UNC Healthcare System summed it up nicely. As chief information officer for one of the largest health systems in North Carolina, she knows well the realities of health data and working in an environment where the public and private sectors must collaborate for success with population health.

## ▶ EXTRACT

Population health is not a new concept. It has been part of the fabric of healthcare since the early days when observation patterns across patients led care providers to make better decisions about the care of their patients. What's exciting and relatively new is that in this era of Electronic Health Records (EHRs) we now have data—and lots of it—to use for gaining new knowledge about the health of populations. This knowledge can be combined with socioeconomic data to create game-changing insights into how people think and act about health, wellness, and lifestyle. Data and analytics connect the circle of population health and individualized care providing a foundation for giant leaps in the health care industry. Data ownership, standardization, privacy, cost, and analytics are some of the challenges facing decision makers around the use of big data to advance healthcare policy. However, in the end, it becomes a very personal motivation when we realize that doing good things with data means helping improve the lives of everyone.

Tracy Parham, RN, BC, MSN, Chief Information Officer: UNC Health Care System

## Medicaid Management

While population health relies heavily on many factors that the government has little direct control over, the government does have much broader control over Medicaid. Medicaid had only begun to really take shape when I was a part of that system as a young child and it has since matured greatly. Medicaid is now the second-largest insurance program in the nation by way of expenditures, over $550 billion in 2015,[12] and the largest by way of enrollment, which has grown to monumental heights with June 2016 numbers at over 70 million.[13] It is traditionally one of the single largest expenditures in state budgets and the supporting-technology infrastructure is one of a state's most costly IT investments.

Further complicating things, studies show Medicaid to be correlated with sicker populations. A 2013 Gallup study shows that Medicaid members, as compared to those in employer-sponsored insurance plans, are more likely to suffer from the following chronic conditions (listed in order of most significant to least by percent difference between Medicaid and employer plans): depression, asthma, diabetes, obesity, high blood pressure, heart attack, and high cholesterol.[14] Medicaid also has significantly higher rates of smoking (over 35 percent) and members struggle to find places to exercise, places to buy medicine, and lack the necessary funds for healthcare and medicine.

Finally, access to care is a severe issue with Medicaid. While many Medicaid participants have issues with transportation to and from an appointment, or getting time off from work, the provider pool from which to choose is significantly smaller than other traditional insurance plans (e.g., employer-sponsored plans), with studies suggesting that nearly one-third of all primary care physicians in the United States do not accept new Medicaid patients and over 55 percent of psychiatrists do not.[15]

The massive rise in enrollment and the expansion of Medicaid clearly and understandably brings with it a mountain of challenges such as care access, cost, quality, and effectiveness. The system also collects, processes, and maintains mountains of data within the many state-run Medicaid management information systems (MMIS) and Medicaid managed care organizations, in addition to other social areas (SNAP, TANF, WIC, housing, child and family services, criminal justice, education, etc.). It is important to note, this relationship between the Medicaid population and other social service areas is profound as Medicaid recipients are typically higher social-service utilizers who create a higher total cost of care.[16] In short, Medicaid programs need to concern themselves not with just health-specific data but converged with data from its other social services to provide themselves with a holistic picture of Medicaid recipients and better understand the interdependencies between health and nonhealth Medicaid services.

As states look to provide their Medicaid populations with the very best health and social outcomes, they need to continue to look at innovative and disruptive approaches to leveraging this data to:

- Enhance care access and quality
- Control costs
- Better administer managed care organizations

Advanced analytics plays a key role in holistically analyzing data from these various Medicaid and social sources. Employing real-time advanced predictive analytics and robust data visualization capabilities can deliver the right insight at the right time and enable decision makers across the Medicaid system to participate in a truly integrated, team-based, analytic approach to care delivery.

 **EXTRACT**

Without a doubt, the effectiveness and success of state efforts in the management and improvement of the Medicaid program, including controlling costs, will be greatly enhanced when we make the investment in the technology and advanced analytics for identifying emerging issues and trends, evaluating and adopting the most efficient and effective interventions, and monitoring and projecting and ultimate results.

Lanier Cansler, former Secretary of NC DHHS

## A Team Effort

Medicaid is a collaboration between federal and state government, and the success of employing analytics within the Medicaid system is greatly improved when federal support for state efforts is present.

The Centers for Medicare and Medicaid Services (CMS) plays a significant role in shaping the framework of data and analytics throughout the national healthcare ecosystem. As administrators of the two largest healthcare payers in the nation, covering over 30 percent of the population,[17] the policy and programs within CMS have profound effects on healthcare providers, payers, and members.[18] CMS consequently possesses perhaps more U.S. health-claim data than nearly any other government or private healthcare organization. With the breadth and maturity of the agencies' data and analytic resources, it has maintained a strong commitment to ensuring that innovative data and analytic initiatives continue to play a prominent role in Medicare and Medicaid programs, and that its members receive access to the highest-quality cost-effective care. CMS has promoted, funded, or directly supported healthcare data and analytic innovation through initiatives that focus on data transparency, such as recent rules to enable broader public access to CMS data, an innovation center (CMMI) focused on supporting strategic federal and state health innovation programs, and performing enhanced analysis on its own data to identify new trends as well as potential fraud, waste, and abuse within the system.

▶ **EXTRACT**

Big data and big analytics brings with it big responsibility. We at CMS are sitting on a treasure trove of health data and have a responsibility to ensure this data is transparent, analyzed, and being responsibly used for the good of our agency, our providers, and healthcare consumers across the nation. Our commitment to innovation is unwavering and we will continue to steadfastly support states, researchers, and the public at large in healthcare data transparency and analytics in the hope we can create healthier, cost-effective outcomes for all.

Niall Brennan, Former CMS Chief Data Officer

Additionally, other CMS initiatives that foster data and analytics include:

- MITA (Medicaid Information Technology Architecture). CMS defines this as "A national framework to support improved systems development and healthcare management for the Medicaid enterprise. MITA has a number of goals, including development of seamless and integrated systems that communicate effectively through interoperability and common standards." It operates as a comprehensive set of guidelines, sort of a blueprint, for states to make better use of their massive investment in Medicaid-technology systems. It supports a foundation of data and paves the way for implementing strong analytics in the Medicaid system.

- Medicaid waivers allow states the opportunity to test and demonstrate innovative ways to manage and pay for services within the Medicaid system. Recent examples include implementing managed care programs, management of complex, high-cost patients, and delivery-system reform efforts that focus on various items like integration of behavioral, physical, and social service care delivery, hospital readmission reduction, and other reforms. States like Washington, California, and New York have recently used these waivers to implement delivery system reforms with strong commitments to data and analytics.

- Policy changes, such as MACRA, that while aimed at Medicare also have significant effects on Medicaid (since many providers participate in both) and pave the way for a system more aligned with value-based payments and consolidation of several incentive initiatives. Medicaid Managed Care (CMS 2390) overhauled the Medicaid managed care system and provides more accountability for MCOs, state oversight of MCOs, and pushes toward more value-based payments and a resultant reduction in fraud, waste, and abuse.

These initiatives and organizations above are meant to ensure that a state's Medicaid technology is modern, modular, flexible, and scalable to enhance the state's efforts to provide their Medicaid population with access to the highest-quality, most effective care while mitigating cost. As states look to enhance their Medicaid systems and participate in initiatives with federal support, it is imperative that they look to invest in and strengthen their data analytics across the enterprise, including Medicaid management/managed care oversight, payment reform, health outcomes, and program integrity. These investments will provide Medicaid stakeholders with the information they need to ensure a more effective/efficient Medicaid program with healthier outcomes.

Examples of Medicaid-management analytics that can be employed include:

- Identify and analyze high-cost, high-utilization patient types (termed hot spotting or superutilizers). How important is this? Five percent of the entire Medicaid population accounts for roughly 50 percent of the entire Medicaid program cost.[19]
- Analyze Medicaid claims data to quickly identify patterns, like provider overutilization, and prevent costs from escalating, or identify quality trends, like higher rates of diabetes in certain regions where access to nutritious meals is problematic, and address these before they become larger issues.
- Provide enhanced managed-care oversight including analysis (and projections where applicable) of outcomes, medical loss ratio (MLR), rate review, benefits, and network adequacy. As new legislation calls for stronger oversight of Medicaid MCOs, it is key for Medicaid programs to support their goals using data and analytics.

■ Identify strategic policy, program, and care interventions while measuring their effectiveness with regards to quality and cost. For example, would expanded funding for a diabetes prevention program equate to better outcomes and long-term financial cost mitigation? Does a short-term increase in specialist care hours for kids in early intervention programs lead to better outcomes? Is one treatment plan more effective than another and how can we learn and replicate?

The state of Alabama's Medicaid program utilizes analytics to help improve quality and control costs.[20] From Alabama Medical Director Dr. Robert Moon. "Our goal is to capture and analyze data to better inform the use of Medicaid's limited resources, but also to drive healthcare quality improvement as a part of our overall transformation process." Dr. Moon also states, "What we have been able to do is to turn data into information that can drive quality decisions and achieve better health outcomes. It can help answer questions like, what is the effect of using evidence-based medicine to drive policy? How does the state's prior authorization policy influence outcomes? Does the utilization of other drugs go up?"

Medicaid administrators are quickly realizing that using superior, enterprise-wide analytics within a single environment provides the ability to understand the complex interdependencies that drive medical outcomes and costs, giving users across the Medicaid spectrum the information they need to improve healthcare and provide a more systemic and comprehensive approach to care.

 **EXTRACT**

While progress has been substantial, states and their partners must remain committed to long term and sustained efforts to build and refine data analytics capacity in order for data-driven decision making to become a permanent feature in Medicaid programs.[21]

National Association of Medicaid Directors

## VALUE-BASED CARE

 **EXTRACT**

PricewaterhouseCoopers estimates $312 billion in clinical waste occurs annually, highlighted by defensive medicine ($210 billion) and potentially avoidable hospital readmits ($25 billion). PricewaterhouseCoopers' Health Research Institute, The Price of Excess: Identifying Waste in Healthcare, 2008, http://www.oss.net/ dynamaster/file_archive/080509/59f26a38c114f2295757bb6be522128a/The%20 Price%20of%20Excess%20-%20Identifying%20Waste%20in%20Healthcare%20 Spending%20-%20PWC.pdf

One of the single largest fundamental flaws of the U.S. healthcare system has been its reliance on incentivizing and operating a healthcare system based primarily on volume instead of on value. Recall earlier points made in this chapter where I spoke of the hefty cost of healthcare in the United States, the lack of growth in global healthcare metrics like life expectancy, and the challenge with finding quality providers and measuring them. Transitioning to a system that relies on performance and rewards more on performance than pure volume has and will continue to cause disruption in the healthcare market and is also a key ingredient to the success of Medicaid management and population health. With research (2015) showing about 40 percent of the country participating in some type of value-based payment program, it is clear that we are moving in that direction but with much room for growth and maturity.[22]

Governments are struggling to do more with less in their health programs (e.g., Medicaid, Medicare, VA, government employee health plans) and are tasked with ensuring their members get access to high-quality care for a fair price, and that providers are held financially accountable for the care they deliver. In addition, the government plays a significant role in ensuring policies and programs are in place that motivate and guide the private healthcare market toward one based on value while also receiving access to high-quality care, at a fair price.

To do this, government healthcare efforts can look to payment reform analytics that can help them better understand the full picture of healthcare—including outcomes and costs—and manage quality across the full continuum of care.

For government health programs, and the broader payer and provider environment, this means analyzing massive volumes of complex health data. This must be done in order to understand the true total cost of care while accounting for various risk-adjusted factors specific to a patient. While the healthcare system, in many people's eyes, including my own, still predominantly is centered on volume not value, efforts to better manage costs have been around for some time. Government and commercial payers, as well as providers alike, have explored and employed a variety of payment management concepts/models over time, including: diagnostic-related groupers (that focus primarily on inpatient hospital stays), all patient-refined, diagnosis-related groups (that adjust for illness severity and mortality risk), patient/provider incentive programs, shared-risk contracts (having providers share in the potential financial risk of a patient), accountable care organizations (a collaborative of many service providers and facilities working together to provide higher-quality care), and much more. The good news is we are making progress as these types of initiatives continue to exist and evolve. The challenging news is when it comes to value-based care, significantly more can be done, including enhancements to many of the concepts above, through analyzing the quality and cost of care at a comprehensive level that a clinical episode of care provides. The clinical episode of care definitions act as guides for describing the rules for why an episode of care exists. A knee replacement, for example, will have rules in the episode definition that encompass all of the care provided for that particular clinical episode including: imaging, orthopedic visits, surgery, physical therapy, and certain prescriptions, all falling within a specific time frame (say six months for knee replacement). All of this care is collectively part of the knee replacement episode. This level of granularity is tremendously valuable as there is now a picture of all the points of care, associated providers, and costs for the patient throughout an episode. However, the definition of an episode, itself, lacks the value that can be realized when combined and enhanced with advanced analytics.

Let's explore some of the vital features a payment-reform initiative should consider when employing an approach with an episode of care-based analytics.

## Inclusive

Includes and analyzes all the clinically relevant care provided (both inpatient and outpatient care) to a patient. If we are going to comprehensively analyze the costs and quality of care and try to positively impact both, then the approach to value analysis must include all points of care. This way we can understand the impact from one point of care to the next. For example a diabetic patient may see several providers—primary care, endocrinologist, cardiologist, and ophthalmologist—and to truly understand the cost of a diabetes episode for this one patient we need to cover all care received, relevant to diabetes, from each point of care. This way providers can better understand how treatments are most successful/not successful, where complications may occur, and how to be more preventative. As a payer or government organization I would also benefit from knowing my analysis covers all the care provided, so I am truly looking at the total cost of care.

## Risk Adjustment

Risk adjusting for patient severity is important as all patients are different and risk adjustment ensures a fair representation of each patient. For example: Two male diabetic patients of similar age and weight may greatly differ and this can have a significant impact on their treatments and costs. While one patient may suffer from comorbidities and be of different racial descent, the other may live in a different region and come from a different financial class. These variables all must be considered when trying to make a fair assessment of care provided. The process of risk adjustment recalibrates the cost of care for each of the patients, and by using analytics helps us to understand whether the cost of care was truly variable or not. This is not only valuable for government policy makers and program administrators as they look to ensure they have an accurate portrait of the cost and variation of care, but also for providers to have a fair assessment when true mitigating factors are present that they may have little control over.

## Episodic Association

Analyzing the clinical associations between multiple episodes of care helps us to see if one episode of care is a result of, or a part of, the same family of episodes. For instance, a patient who suffers from cardiac arrest may very likely also have had a bypass surgery and be diabetic. Each one is an episode. It is vital to understand that all three may be associated and have impacts on each other. Some may look at the heart attack and bypass and just combine those episodes because they are from the same family of clinical care, while being a diabetic may possibly indicate that the heart attack was part of that episode as well and would also be associated. This is important, as it helps us to understand the breadth of care that is provided to a patient, and how care quality and cost from one episode can be impacted by another. Furthermore, this association process provides an inherent quality evaluation of providers, since the process evaluates if patients are receiving the typical care for that episode and how other episodes may have resulted from poor care. For all involved in the healthcare system, this provides an alternative to national quality measures such as HEDIS, which have traditionally not been tied to total cost or taken into account the comprehensive clinical details an episode provides, and allows all involved to better understand the relationship between quality and cost.

## Cost Components

Calculating the various cost components associated with an episode helps create an even more accurate picture of the costs associated with care down to the episodic level, including comparing the actual cost of care to the risk-adjusted cost, and to other costs such as typical (what is the typical cost of the care?) and potentially avoidable costs (PACs). PACs are an area of significant impact. Think of the estimated $312 billion in annual clinical waste (including preventable hospital readmits, defensive medicine, medical errors and more) that PricewaterhouseCoopers estimated and consider the possibilities if these costs were able to be better analyzed and more importantly prevented. If we think about the previous example with a patient who had the heart attack, a bypass, and is diabetic, wouldn't it be good to know if the diabetes was poorly controlled and perhaps led to the heart attack? Or, whether there were associated hospital readmissions because the same patient acquired an infection while in the hospital? With the combination of employing a clinical episode of care and understanding the associations and PACs, patients' costs could either be justified or investigated and providers held fiscally accountable for the poor quality of care that led to the heart attack or readmission or other association. If these are clinically avoidable then the reasonable question is: Shouldn't hospitals and providers involved perhaps share in the cost of that complication instead of payers, government, and patients? Additionally, an opportunity exists for those facilities and providers that are operating with the highest-quality care to share those best practices with others through the power of data and analytics. Finally, this enables fiscal healthcare agents, like insurance payers and government organizations such as Medicaid/Medicare, the opportunity to refine value-based payment models, such as bundled payments and other incentive-based payment methodologies, based on enriched episode analytics to better understand any potential financial risk.

## ▶ EXTRACT

During one analytic study involving a state Medicaid data set covering approximately 100k patients and 2 years of data, the study found over $100 million in potentially avoidable complications costs representing over 25 percent of the allocated costs of episode care (Figure 4.3).

# EPISODE OVERVIEW

## POV Episode Overview:  Note PAC% of 29.9% ($113,258,389)

| All Members ◄ | Allocated IP | Allocated OP | Allocated FPO | Allocated Total | PAC | % PAC | Percent Allocated | Total Paid |
|---|---|---|---|---|---|---|---|---|
| All Members | $99,604,984 | $79,978,792 | $199,707,169 | $379,290,944 | $113,258,389 | 29.9% | 47.2% | $804,192,948 |

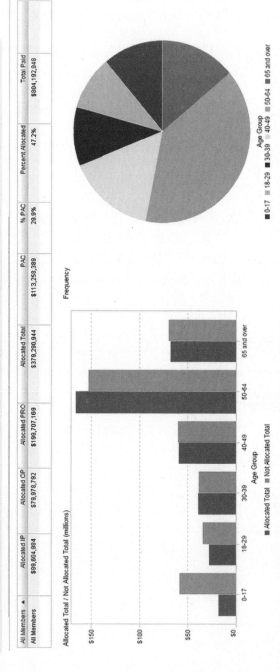

**Figure 4.3** State Medicaid data analysis results show episode costs. Note the over $113 million in potentially avoidable costs.

## Cost Allocation

Since episode analytics are based on claims, and most value-based payment methodologies are also sourced from claims, cost allocation is vital. A single healthcare claim can have multiple services listed and if the claim is not properly analyzed, costs could accidentally be attributed in their entirety to one provider who should not be responsible. Therefore, it is important to understand how to allocate the services provided from a single claim across multiple relevant episodes, while also providing a provider attribution methodology to ensure the appropriate provider is being assigned. This enables the benefit of accurately measuring the quality of care by attributing all relevant services provided to the appropriate provider and avoiding under- or overrepresenting costs of episodes due to lost services that aren't split and counted toward the appropriate episodes. This is particularly important to get a true picture of costs associated with an episode and provider while ensuring that providers are comfortable with the service-assignment methodology and that the claim service-assignment process is fair and representative.

## Prescriptive Analytics

As value-based payment initiatives become more and more prevalent, organizations will want to analyze not only the past but also plan for the future. Advanced predictive analytics capabilities within an episode-analytic environment can be very powerful and provide incredible insight into:

- Patient-level risk scoring for future potentially avoidable complications and high costs (and ask how can we prevent and plan for these).
- Strategic interventions with payment incentives, policy, programs, and even treatment that might mitigate these costs and increase quality of care.
- Forecast how payment models might perform in the future and also look at which variables may impact the performance of

these models and optimize the models ahead of time to ensure the models are performing at a high level.

- Looking beyond clinical data and better understanding/ predicting the impact between non-health services and Episodes.

While Episode based initiatives have taken steps forward (by many payers, providers, and CMS) broader and more analytically driven approaches to Episodes of Care can be instrumental for governments, payers, and providers to better understand the quality and cost of care, as well as how to develop, maintain, and continue to enhance value-based payment arrangements, such as bundled payments and other risk-sharing methodologies based on clinical episodes of care. Ultimately they are another key ingredient to successfully move toward 100 percent value-based healthcare in the United States.

## CONCLUSION

Healthcare in the United States has come a long way, from before my time when there was little or no technology, to the beginnings of it when I was just a child, to where we are today in the midst of a full health information technology movement. When I began my journey in 1977 there was little or no use of data and analytics to support healthcare decisions across the system, but as I write these words I reflect admirably on the progress this nation has made with health information technology and on my passion for evangelizing the tremendous value that data and analytics can have to support people like myself with a path to healthier living. As this movement continues to take shape, the government must embrace its role as a leader in healthcare data and analytics, collaborate with the private sector, seek feedback from the public, and continue supporting data and analytic innovation through its complex and influential role with healthcare policy, programs, providers, and payers. Doing so will help to ensure that current and future generations are the beneficiaries of what could possibly be the greatest healthcare system in the world.

## NOTES

1. Zika Virus Fact Sheet, World Health Organization (September 6, 2016), www.who.int/mediacentre/factsheets/zika/en/.

2. Jerry White, "Life Expectancy Gap Between US Rich and Poor Widens," Global Research, Centre for Research on Globalization (April 12, 2016), www.globalresearch.ca/life-expectancy-gap-between-us-rich-and-poor-widens/5519885.

3. Mortality Data, National Center for Health Statistics, National Vital Statistics System, Centers for Disease Control and Prevention, www.cdc.gov/nchs/nvss/deaths.htm.

4. National Health Expenditure Projections 2015–2025, Centers for Medicare and Medicaid Services (July 2016), www.cms.gov/Research-Statistics-Data-and-Systems/Statistics-Trends-and-Reports/NationalHealthExpendData/NationalHealthAccountsProjected.html.

5. Raj Chetty, Michael Stepner, Sarah Abraham, Shelby Lin, Benjamin Scuderi, Nicholas Turner, Augustin Bergeron, and David Cutler, "The Association Between Income and Life Expectancy in the United States, 2001–2014," *The JAMA Network* (April 26, 2016), http://jamanetwork.com/journals/jama/article-abstract/2513561.

6. Steven A. Schroeder, "We Can Do Better—Improving the Health of the American People," *The New England Journal of Medicine* (September 20, 2007), www.nejm.org/doi/full/10.1056/nejmsa073350#t=article.

7. *The Digital Universe: Driving Data Growth in Healthcare—Challenges & Opportunities for IT,* EMC Digital Universe, www.emc.com/analyst-report/digital-universe-healthcare-vertical-report-ar.pdf.

8. Julian Bunn, "How Big is a Petabyte, Exabyte, Zettabyte, or a Yottabyte?" *High Scalability Blog* (September 11, 2012), http://highscalability.com/blog/2012/9/11/how-big-is-a-petabyte-exabyte-zettabyte-or-a-yottabyte.html.

9. Satish Misra, "New Report Finds More Than 165,000 Mobile Health Apps Now Available, Takes Close Look at Characteristics and Use," *iMedicalApps.com* (September 17, 2015), www.imedicalapps.com/2015/09/ims-health-apps-report/#.

10. The Office of the National Coordinator for Health Information Technology, "Health Care Professionals HER Vendors," *Healthit.gov*, Health IT Dashboard, Quick-Stats

(July 2016), http://dashboard.healthit.gov/quickstats/pages/FIG-Vendors-of-EHRs -to-Participating-Professionals.php.

11. Northeastern University, "Population Health Investments by Health Plans and Large Provider Organizations – Exploring the Business Case," Northeastern University Institute on Urban Health Research and Practice (March 2016), www.northeastern .edu/iuhrp/wp-content/uploads/2016/05/PopHealthBusinessCaseFullRpt-5-1.pdf.

12. Sylvia Mathews Burwell, "2016 Actuarial Report on the Financial Outlook for Medicaid," Office of the Actuary, Centers for Medicare and Medicaid Services. U.S. Department of Health and Human Services (2016), www.medicaid.gov/medicaid/ financing-and-reimbursement/downloads/medicaid-actuarial-report-2016.pdf.

13. National Medicaid and CHIP Program Information, "Medicaid and CHIP: May and June 2016 Monthly Enrollment Updated August 2016," Medicaid.gov (2016), https://www.medicaid.gov/medicaid/program-information/medicaid-and-chip -enrollment-data/index.html.

14. Elizabeth Mendes, "Preventable Chronic Conditions Plague Medicaid Population," Gallup.com (April 4, 2013), www.gallup.com/poll/161615/preventable-chronic -conditions-plague-medicaid-population.aspx.

15. Sandra L. Deceker, "Two-Thirds of Primary Care Physicians Accepted New Medicaid Patients in 2011–2012: A Baseline to Measure Future Acceptance Rates," *Health Affairs*, content.healthaffairs.org/content/32/7/1183.full.

16. Ari Gottlieb, "The Still Expanding State of Medicaid in the United States," PWC. com, (November 2015), www.pwc.com/us/en/healthcare/publications/assets/ pwc-the-still-expanding-state-of-medicaid-in-the-united-states.pdf.

17. U.S. and World Population Clock, https://www.census.gov/popclock/.

18. Medicare Enrollment Dashboard, https://www.cms.gov/Research-Statistics-Data -and-Systems/Statistics-Trends-and-Reports/Dashboard/Medicare-Enrollment/ Enrollment%20Dashboard.html.

19. Peter Sullivan, "5 Percent of Medicaid Patients Account for Half of Program's Costs," The Hill.com (May 8, 2015), http://thehill.com/policy/healthcare/241491-5 -percent-of-medicaid-patients-account-for-50-percent-of-costs.

20. Alabama Medicaid, "New Technology Helps Drive Quality Improvement and Cost-Savings. Alabama Medicaid," http://medicaid.alabama.gov/news_detail .aspx?ID=8798.

21. National Association of Medicaid Directors, "Data Analytics for Effective Reform: How State Medicaid Agencies Are Leveraging Data for Payment and Delivery System Innovation," *Issue Brief* (April 2014), http://medicaiddirectors.org/wp-content/ uploads/2015/08/data_analytics_for_effective_reform_1.pdf.

22. Health Care Transformation Task Force, "Health Care Transformation Task Force Reports Increase in Value-Based Payments," Press Release (April 12, 2016), http://hcttf.org/releases/2016/4/12/healthcare-transformation-task-force-reports -increase-in-value-based-payments.

# CHAPTER 5

# Prescription Drug Abuse

*Steve Kearney*

## INTRODUCTION

I n July 2016, the National Governors Association (NGA) released a
Compact to Fight Opioid Addiction signed by 46 governors. This was
the first time in more than 10 years that the NGA had worked on and
released guidance on such an issue. The press release stated, "By signing
the compact, governors are agreeing to redouble their efforts to fight
the opioid epidemic with new steps to reduce inappropriate prescribing, change the nation's understanding of opioids and addiction, and
ensure a pathway to recovery for individuals suffering from addiction."
The Compact was necessary due to the overwhelming epidemic that is
now prevalent in all states. According to the Centers for Disease Control
and Prevention (CDC), "The United States is in the midst of an opioid
overdose epidemic. Opioids (including prescription opioid pain reliev-
ers and heroin) killed more than 33,000 people in 2015, more than
any year on record. At least half of all opioid overdose deaths involve
a prescription opioid. Ninety-one Americans die every day from an opioid
overdose."[1] That is one person dying every 15 minutes. This insidious
problem has been growing since the late 1990s. I sat in Grand Rounds
at Duke (the internal education sessions for providers) and distinctly
remember case studies and new national guidelines that proposed the
increased use of opioids for chronic non-cancer pain, thinking the U.S.
health system was letting people suffer. Opioids were a solution that
would provide relief and the United States quickly adopted their use
because they were deemed effective by the patients and the providers. Many patients quickly realized the euphoric effects of this type
of treatment, and the health system benefited from satisfied patients
that had previously required a great deal of resources both in time and
money. Think physical therapy, cognitive therapy, and intense evaluation versus giving the patient a quick-fix pill. Unfortunately, patients
were lulled into a false sense of security, that these medications must be
okay because they were prescribed for them by their doctor, and supported by national guidelines. Pain became the Fifth Vital Sign. Providers thought they were doing what was best for their patients and it was
supported by their peers and experts in the field.

Unfortunately, the use became pervasive and problems with addiction began to rise. Employees who were injured returned to work with

pills that could keep their pain in check and allow them to function. Athletes were provided pain relief after surgery that many times continued throughout extended physical rehab and resulted in profound addiction. It became the norm for any type of pain—dental, orthopedic, chronic back, fibromyalgia, rheumatoid arthritis, to name a few, to be treated all with the same therapy. Longer acting and stronger opioids were needed and developed. The cycle continued and has now reached the point that every person, every city, every town, every state government and the entire country has been affected. A new study has also demonstrated the disastrous financial burden to all states and the country as a whole. Florence et al. have estimated the impact on the U.S. economy at $78.5 billion based on 2013 data.[2] The criminal justice burden alone is estimated to be close to $7.7 billion. This epidemic costs lives and a tremendous amount of money. The NGA working group provided additional details under each of the main areas to assist states in their efforts.

With this compact, the undersigned commit to build on their efforts to fight opioid addiction by

- Taking steps to reduce inappropriate opioid prescribing, which may include:
  - Partnering with health care providers to develop or update evidence-based opioid prescribing guidelines, which may be informed by CDC's guideline, and consider prescription limits with exceptions for certain patients and circumstances;
  - Requiring that physicians, osteopaths, nurse practitioners, physician assistants, dentists, veterinarians and all other opioid prescribers receive education on pain management, opioid prescribing, and addiction throughout their training and careers;
  - Integrating data from state prescription drug monitoring programs (PDMPs) into electronic health records and requiring PDMP use by opioid prescribers and dispensers; and
  - Reducing payment and administrative barriers in Medicaid and other health plans to promote comprehensive pain management that includes alternatives to opioid painkillers.

- Leading efforts to change the nation's understanding of opioids and addiction, which may include:
  - Developing a communications strategy through the governor's office to raise awareness about the risks of abuse associated with opioid use and reduce the stigma of addiction;
  - Establishing social media campaigns and integrating education into schools, athletic programs and other community-based settings to raise awareness about opioid abuse and addiction among youth and other at-risk groups; and
  - Partnering with professional associations to improve understanding of the disease of addiction among health care providers and law enforcement.
- Taking actions to ensure a pathway to recovery for individuals with addiction, which may include:
  - Reducing payment and administrative barriers in Medicaid and other health plans to promote access to a range of treatment options, including well-supervised, medication-assisted treatment and comprehensive recovery services;
  - Pursuing overdose prevention and harm reduction strategies, such as Good Samaritan laws and standing orders to increase access to and use of naloxone; and
  - Implementing and strengthening programs that provide addiction treatment as an alternative for nonviolent individuals charged with low-level drug-related crimes.[3]

The NGA should be commended on their efforts. The states will need all of these initiatives and more to address this problem. These focus areas have several things in common:

1. They all involve a tremendous amount of data that can be used to help solve this problem.
2. They all will require agencies to work together to coordinate and share this data to understand the problem and ways to address it in an unprecedented fashion.
3. They have the opportunity to determine where the next problems are going to arise if these initiatives are set up with the end in mind and focus on analytics.

## NATIONAL INITIATIVES

In March 2015, Secretary for Health and Human Services Sylvia M. Burwell announced a new major initiative aimed at addressing the opioid epidemic. The following focus areas are from the press release:

1. Providing training and educational resources, including updated prescriber guidelines, to assist health professionals in making informed prescribing decisions and address the over-prescribing of opioids.

2. Increasing use of naloxone, as well as continuing to support the development and distribution of the life-saving drug, to help reduce the number of deaths associated with prescription opioid and heroin overdose.

3. Expanding the use of Medication-Assisted Treatment (MAT), a comprehensive way to address the needs of individuals that combines the use of medication with counseling and behavioral therapies to treat substance use disorders.

As part of these priority areas, the secretary's efforts build on current HHS strategies to address the opioid epidemic and expands many of the most promising initiatives with the greatest potential for impact, including:

Helping health professionals to make the most informed prescribing decisions:

- Teaching medical professionals how and when to prescribe opioids by working with lawmakers on bipartisan legislation requiring specific training for safe opioid prescribing and establishing new opioid prescribing guidelines for chronic pain.

- Supporting data sharing for safe prescribing by facilitating prescription drug monitoring programs (PDMP) and health information technology integration and further adoption of electronic prescribing practices.

- Increasing investments in state-level prevention interventions, including PDMPs, to track opioid prescribing and support appropriate pain management.

Increasing use of naloxone:

- Supporting the development, review, and approval of new naloxone products and delivery options.
- Promoting state use of Substance Abuse Block Grant funds to purchase naloxone.
- Implementing the Prescription Drug Overdose grant program for states to purchase naloxone and train first responders on its use.

Expanding use of Medication-Assisted Treatment (MAT):

- Launching a grant program in FY 2015 to improve access to MAT services through education, training, and purchase of MAT medications for treatment of prescription opioid and heroin addiction.
- Exploring bipartisan policy changes to increase use of buprenorphine and develop the training to assist prescribing.[4]

This announcement came in addition to the announcement on March 6, 2015, that the CDC launched the Prescription Drug Overdose Prevention for States program.

The program provided 16 state health departments resources to enhance their prescription drug monitoring programs and to advance prevention efforts. An additional 13 states were funded in March 2016 to bring the total to 29 states as part of the program. The federal government now has an unprecedented number of agencies working on this epidemic. Listed below are the agencies and some of their current initiatives:

Centers for Disease Control and Prevention (CDC)

> Guideline for Prescribing Opioids for Chronic Pain Prevention for States Program—29 states funded $50 million

> Data-Driven Prevention Initiative—13 states funded $18 million

> Enhanced State Surveillance—12 states funded $12.8 million

Substance Abuse and Mental Health Services Administration (SAMHSA)

> Substance Abuse and Mental Health Block Grants

> Naloxone Funding and First Responder Training

The Office of National Drug Control Policy

> High Intensity Drug Trafficking Areas (HIDTAs)

Department of Justice (DOJ)

> Harold Rogers Grants for PDMPs—49 states have received startup funds

> COPS Anti-Heroin Task Force Program

Department of Agriculture (USDA)

> Rural Health and Safety Education Program (Telemedicine)

> Community Facilities Grants and Loans Program

> Rural Housing Program for Individuals in Recovery

Federal Drug Administration (FDA)

The FDA has committed to the following changes to address the opioid epidemic:

- Reexamine the risk–benefit paradigm for opioids and ensure that the agency considers their wider public health effects.
- Convene an expert advisory committee before approving any new drug application for an opioid that does not have abuse deterrent properties.
- Assemble and consult with the Pediatric Advisory Committee regarding a framework for pediatric opioid labeling before any new labeling is approved.
- Develop changes to immediate release opioid labeling, including additional warnings and safety information that incorporate elements similar to the extended release/long acting (ER/LA) opioid analgesics labeling that is currently required.
- Update risk evaluation and mitigation strategy requirements for opioids after considering advisory committee recommendations and review of existing requirements.
- Expand access to, and encourage the development of, abuse deterrent formulations of opioid products.
- Improve access to naloxone and MAT options for patients with opioid use disorders.
- Support better pain management options, including alternative treatments.

Secretary Burwell's focus on helping health professionals to make the most informed prescribing decisions includes focusing on data sharing through prescription drug monitoring programs, health information technology integration, and adoption of electronic prescribing practices.

## PRESCRIPTION DRUG MONITORING PROGRAMS

Prescription drug monitoring programs have been in existence since 1939, when California set up the first program to monitor Schedule II medications. Medications are placed in categories or schedules based on their acceptable medical use and their potential for abuse or dependency. There are currently five Schedules—Schedule I through Schedule V, with I being no medical use and the most abuse potential. The early programs used multipage forms that sent a copy of the information to the program that was collecting the information. By 1989 there were nine programs in existence and they were housed under various state agencies:

Attorney General's Office—California 1939 and Pennsylvania 1972

Public Safety—Hawaii 1943 and Texas 1981

Bureau of Narcotics—New York 1970 and Rhode Island 1978

Substance Abuse Services—Illinois 1961

Board of Pharmacy—Idaho 1967

Bureau of Health Professions—Michigan 1988

The DEA and the programs operating at the time developed the Alliance of States with prescription drug monitoring programs in 1990. This alliance facilitated the exchange of information and also transitioned from the paper forms to a computerized database. Oklahoma (1990) and Massachusetts (1992) were some of the first to collect the information in an electronic format. They also started collecting all of the scheduled prescriptions. Nevada developed a PDMP in 1997 that was housed in the Board of Pharmacy and became the first to provide data directly to pharmacists and prescribers. To date, 49 states, the District of Columbia, and the Territory of Guam have some form of prescription drug monitoring program (PDMP). Missouri continues to be the only state that does not have a program.

The basic premise of the current prescription drug monitoring programs (PDMPs) are to collect the scheduled drug data from pharmacies and dispensing providers, house that data in a standard format, and make the data available through a user interface so that information can be consumed. Many times the agency that administers the PDMP then sets the direction for the use of the information.

If the PDMP is under the direction of the Department of Justice within a state then the initial focus usually was on law enforcement and ways to ensure that controlled substances were not being used illegally or that prescribers and dispensers were not using controlled substances as a way for financial gain. Chairman Harold Rogers of the House Appropriations Committee established a competitive grant program in 2001 within the Department of Justice that helped to stimulate the growth of these programs. I have been very fortunate to meet with Chairman Rogers and his team to discuss the role analytics plays in this space, and the new grants include language that support analytics and using other data to provide value. Public health organizations have focused on prevention and reducing prescription drug abuse as the epidemic has taken on a much broader impact, while Boards of Pharmacy, which administer 20 of the programs, have focused on education and a licensing-board approach. I was able to work with Project Lazarus in North Carolina for the past two years on these prevention efforts with community coalitions and helped to develop and participate in the education programs for providers in all 100 counties. The common missing theme in all of these endeavors was actionable data. All of these programs have struggled with the sheer volume of prescriptions, problems with data quality due to manual entry of the information, understaffing, and underfunding.

## ADVANCED ANALYTICS

The current PDMPs are trying extremely hard to meet their remit of getting the data in a format where the end user can evaluate it.

I have been very fortunate to travel across the United States and meet with many of the PDMP administrators to discuss ways that the systems can be improved.

They all cite the same problems of spending the majority of their time trying to get the data in a consumable format, or having to manually develop ways to answer questions from legislators, providers, public health, law enforcement, consumers, and so on.

If we go back to our premise in the introduction of the book regarding analytics and the specific stages—analytic hindsight (what has happened), insight (what is causing this to happen), and foresight (how we can intervene and optimize outcomes). The current PDMPs focus on hindsight. Collecting the data, doing descriptive statistics on the data, and providing a way to share the data. They are so underfunded and understaffed that it is difficult to keep up with all of the requests from different agencies, the reports for grant requirements, and the resolution of data problems. Many have a difficult time trying to provide analytics because they are focused on keeping the system operational and meeting their original remit to their sponsoring agencies. The feedback from providers has been that the systems are too difficult to use and they take too much time. In fact, in a national survey of 1,000 primary care providers, 72 percent were aware that their state had a PDMP, but only 380 of the providers had actually used the program.[5]

The actionable part of the story is where we need to focus. What would make providers, legislators, licensing boards, public health entities, and so on take action? To do that, you need to start with the basics. Develop a data approach that ensures you have the right patient and the right provider. The current systems have challenges with patient identity. Bring in other data sets to add more value to the system. For example: A patient can be admitted to the hospital for opioid overdose, be discharged from the hospital, and then go to their local pharmacy and get another prescription for opioids filled.

The pharmacy would not know that the patient has just been in the hospital and the addicted patient is not going to tell them. The provider does not gain any value from the system unless they log in to the system and actively search for their patient or patients. We need a new way to approach systematic change. Providers want—and the Office of the National Coordinator (ONC) agrees with them—the PDMP data incorporated into electronic medical records. A number of states are working on various pilots for this type of data integration.

Unfortunately, this is a slow process and at the end of the day if it is not incorporated correctly and with additional data sources, it still may be of limited value to the provider. Not only do we need advanced analytics, we need disruptive data and analytics. The reporting and descriptive statistics that take up a tremendous amount of the time and effort for most PDMPs should be automated. Solicited reports (those requested by agencies, providers, law enforcement, etc.) should be readily available in an automated queue for access through a self-service user interface based on log-in credentials and data use agreements between agencies. Providers, pharmacies, licensing boards, law enforcement, and so on should be provided automated, unsolicited reports with benchmarking based on peer group by specialty, geography, and cost. These reports should also include actionable data such as emergency room visits, naloxone administration, hospitalizations, and, in worst-case scenarios, deaths. We have the technology and expertise to send this information within 24 hours to agencies, providers, pharmacies, and coalitions that would act on it. We then need to focus on taking what we learn from all of this information to determine the next stage, which would be insights (what is causing this to happen?). This takes organizations that are used to big-data approaches to problems and have the expertise to analyze all of the data in real time to determine actionable insights.

## HEALTH OUTCOMES

In many instances, conversations about health outcomes become an academic exercise. I have worked in the field for more than 20 years and have seen projects stall due to the fact they don't have a true project goal or measureable outcome. This is not the case for the prescription drug abuse/opioid epidemic. If it took you more than 15 minutes to read this chapter another person died in the United States. If you put this book down and picked it up the next day, 91 people died. We have measurable outcomes in lives saved, resources properly utilized, and law enforcement burden reduced. Efforts to date have begun to identify the problem, but as changes have been made within the prescription opioid problem we have seen the overdoses shift more to heroin. Heroin combined with prescription drugs is a spiral into the abyss. These folks feel abandoned with no way out, no hope for tomorrow, and as a society we are failing them. Addressing outcomes has to start with prescription opioids, but the predictive analytics (foresight) and intervention has to include heroin. Heroin is a much more difficult problem to apply analytics to due to the lack of data currently in the system. New approaches will have to be developed that include data from multiple agencies to help identify trends and to determine interventions based on analyzing that data. Naloxone use and law enforcement data will have to be leveraged to act as surrogate markers for these individuals that are no longer in the system. Heroin, fentanyl, and carfentanyl overdoses demand much more of a bio-surveillance approach and will require traditional data sets to merge with emerging models. Policies will have to be developed that allow agencies to share data as they would for any other national biological threat and, based on my conversations with the Office of National Drug Control Policy, the federal government is already supporting those initiatives.

There are too many stories of children found in the company of unresponsive parents due to this epidemic[6] and of children notifying authorities that they could not wake their parents only to find them dead from an overdose.[7] Too many relatives are having to tell children their mommy or daddy is not coming home. There are organizations out there trying to make a difference but they need resources and data. The approach needs to include prevention and treatment and it all needs to be measured, analyzed, and a path forward determined. Prevention starts with ways to keep patients from prolonged opioid use. Real-time information that keeps the patient from being an acute opioid patient and transitioning to a chronic patient is a must. Treatment is really where data and analytics are needed. The best time to intervene for many of these patients is when they have had an overdose, during an emergency room visit or hospitalization. The data systems need to have an enterprise approach where primary care and substance abuse professionals are made aware in real time of the opportunity to intervene and then they can determine what resources are available for a given area to help the patient.

Think of a running queue for patients as they enter the system through various channels. A care manager can be notified of where a treatment bed or treatment specialist has available capacity and can get the patient in to treatment right away. Also by using this data, states and other parties can identify areas to place resources and measure the outcomes of those treatment centers. The system can use the data to learn and adapt for the best outcomes. States like North Carolina have been working on these types of systems in law enforcement and you will hear about that later in the book. We can apply those same learnings and principles to change the dynamic of this disease. States need to start small and work up to larger solutions. This is a difficult and multipronged epidemic. Many states don't know where to start or have self-imposed restrictions that keep data from being used to change the course of this problem. We need individuals to be bold and to use data and analytics to be disruptive with a positive outcome. Even though it is a daunting task, we can't delay. We have to do something within the next 15 minutes.

**PROFILE**

**Steve Kearney,** PharmD, is medical director for US government at SAS Institute. Dr. Kearney works with a world-renowned team to help solve the most complex healthcare challenges by utilizing advanced analytical solutions. Prior to joining SAS, he was a director in the medical outcomes specialists group for Pfizer Global Medical where he worked for 17 years integrating clinical, HIT, health outcomes, and policy for states, integrated delivery networks, payers, providers, and patients. He had a practice at Duke University Medical Center, was faculty and course coordinator at the UNC Eschelman School of Pharmacy for Ambulatory Medicine, and assistant director of the nonaffiliated AHEC at Duke.

## NOTES

1. Rose A. Rudd, Puja Seth, Felicita David, and  Lawrence Scholl, "Increases in Drug and Opioid-Involved Overdose Deaths—United States, 2000–2015," Centers for Disease Control and Prevention (December 30, 2016), www.cdc.gov/mmwr/volumes/65/wr/mm655051e1.htm.

2. Curtis S. Florence, Chao Zhou, Feijun Luo, and Likang Xu, "The Economic Burden of Prescription Opioid Overdose, Abuse, and Dependence in the United States, 2013," *Medical Care* 54, no. 10 (October 2016), http://journals.lww.com/lww-medicalcare/pages/articleviewer.aspx?year=2016&issue=10000&article=00002&type=abstract.

3. National Governors Association, "A Compact to Fight Opioid Addiction" (July 13, 2016), www.nga.org/cms/Compact-to-Fight-Opioid-Addiction.

4. "HHS Takes Strong Steps to Address Opioid-Drug Related Overdose, Death and Dependence," HHS.gov (March 26, 2015), http://wayback.archive-it. org/3926/20170127185704/https://www.hhs.gov/about/news/2015/03/26/ hhs-takes-strong-steps-to-address-opioid-drug-related-overdose-death-and -dependence.html.

5. Lainie Rutkow, Lydia Turner, Eleanor Lucas, Catherine Hwang, and G. Caleb Alexander, "Most Primary Care Physicians Are Aware of Prescription Drug Monitoring Programs, But Many Find the Data Difficult to Access," Health Affairs.org (March 2015), content.healthaffairs.org/content/34/3/484.abstract.

6. Christopher Ingraham and Carolyn Y. Johnson, "Ohio City Shares Shocking Photos of Adults Who Overdosed With a Small Child in the Car," *The Washington Post*, September 9, 2016, https://www.washingtonpost.com/news/wonk/wp/2016/09/09/ ohio-city-shares-shocking-photos-of-adults-who-overdosed-with-a-small-child-in -their-car/.

7. Avianne Tan, "Parents Found Dead After Child Tells School She Couldn't Wake Them Up," ABCNews.go.com (October 5, 2016), http://abcnews.go.com/US/ parents-found-dead-child-tells-school-wake/story?id=42583531.

# CHAPTER 6

# Criminal Justice and Public Safety

*David Kennedy*

The criminal justice and public safety system is connected to almost every facet of government operations. Improvements made in education, child well-being, healthcare, fraud, and prescription drug abuse can help reduce the likelihood that people are involved in the criminal justice system. The justice and public safety community is made up of people who have dedicated their lives to keeping our neighborhoods safe, to protecting our families, and to safeguarding our freedoms. I have spent the past twelve years working with criminal justice and law enforcement agencies. Many of the people I have had the pleasure of working with have dedicated their entire lives to public service. I appreciate the work of all criminal justice practitioners and am proud to count hundreds of them among my colleagues and friends.

It is a challenging time for the U.S. criminal justice and public safety community. Prisons are overcrowded, recidivism rates are high, court systems are congested, and police–community relations are strained (see Figure 6.1).

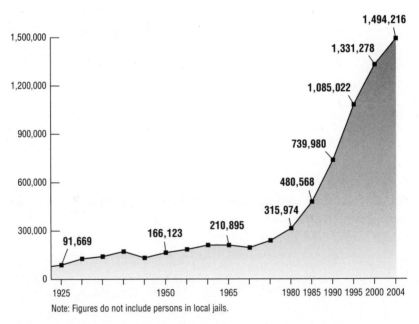

Note: Figures do not include persons in local jails.

**Figure 6.1** Incarcerated Persons in State and Federal Prisons, 1925–2004
*Source: Ryan S. King, Marc Mauer, and Malcolm C. Young, "Incarceration and Crime: A Complex Relationship," The Sentencing Project, 2005, www.sentencingproject.org/wp -content/uploads/2016/01/Incarceration-and-Crime-A-Complex-Relationship.pdf.*

The United States has the highest rate of incarcerated individuals in the world at 716 inmates per 100,000 of the national population.[1] This represents a 700 percent increase over the last four decades according to a 2012 Vera Institute of Justice study.[2] Incarcerated individuals also have increasingly complex issues. According to the Bureau of Prisons, there are over 200,000 inmates housed in state prisons that have a drug crime as their most serious offense. A 2005 Bureau of Justice Statistics report states that "more than half of all prison and jail inmates had a mental health problem."[3] (See Figure 6.2.)

Not surprisingly, the costs associated with imprisonment are staggering and continue to grow. In 2012, the taxpayer burden was $39 billion.[4] This places a financial strain on taxpayers, stresses community resources, and results in other programs being underfunded.

It's clear that our high-cost, traditional approaches to justice and public safety need to be improved. In 1999, a quantitative review of 50 studies involving over 300,000 offenders examined the effect of imprisonment and longer sentences on recidivism. The review indicated that "none of the analyses found imprisonment to reduce recidivism. The recidivism rate for offenders who were imprisoned as opposed to given a community sanction were similar."[5] In other words, incarceration is neither the least costly nor most effective intervention for most people.

In addition, we don't have enough police investigators to solve crimes the traditional, manually intensive way. Justice practitioners are drowning in the data that could help identify alternative approaches but they don't have the skills, tools, or access to be able to leverage it effectively.

The key is realizing that historical data and an analysis of the data can be used throughout the entire criminal justice and public safety process. Data can be used to help law enforcement make better informed decisions about whether to consider diversionary tactics or available social services options. Analysis of past offenders and their individual circumstances can provide valuable insights regarding future bond and pretrial decisions. Jail and prison personnel can better understand which programs most effectively reduce the rate of recidivism based on factors across the inmate population. There is no limit to how the use of analyzed data can help solve the current and future challenges facing our criminal justice and public safety community.

## Highlights

**High prevalence of mental health problems among prison and jail inmates**

| | Percent of inmates in — | | | |
| --- | --- | --- | --- | --- |
| | State prison | | Local jail | |
| Selected characteristics | With mental problem | Without | With mental problem | Without |
| **Criminal record** | | | | |
| Current or past violent offense | 61% | 56% | 44% | 36% |
| 3 or more prior incarcerations | 25 | 19 | 26 | 20 |
| **Substance dependence or abuse** | 74% | 56% | 76% | 53% |
| Drug use in month before arrest | 63% | 49% | 62% | 42% |
| **Family background** | | | | |
| Homelessness in year before arrest | 13% | 6% | 17% | 9% |
| Past physical or sexual abuse | 27 | 10 | 24 | 8 |
| Parents abused alcohol or drugs | 39 | 25 | 37 | 19 |
| **Charged with violating facility rules*** | 58% | 43% | 19% | 9% |
| Physical or verbal assault | 24 | 14 | 8 | 2 |
| **Injured in a fight since admission** | 20% | 10% | 9% | 3% |

*Includes items not shown.

• Nearly a quarter of both State prisoners and jail inmates who had a mental health problem, compared to a fifth of those without, had served 3 or more prior incarcerations.

• Female inmates had higher rates of mental health problems than male inmates (State prisons: 73% of females and 55% of males; local jails: 75% of females and 63% of males).

• About 74% of State prisoners and 76% of local jail inmates who had a mental health problem met criteria for substance dependence or abuse.

• Nearly 63% of State prisoners who had a mental health problem had used drugs in the month before their arrest, compared to 49% of those without a mental health problem.

• State prisoners who had a mental health problem were twice as likely as those without to have been homeless in the year before their arrest (13% compared to 6%).

• Jail inmates who had a mental health problem (24%) were three times as likely as jail inmates without (8%) to report being physically or sexually abused in the past.

• Over 1 in 3 State prisoners and 1 in 6 jail inmates who had a mental health problem had received treatment since admission.

• State prisoners who had a mental health problem were twice as likely as State prisoners without to have been injured in a fight since admission (20% compared to 10%).

**Figure 6.2** High Prevalence of Mental Health Problems among Prison and Jail Inmates
*Source: Doris J. James and Lauren E. Glaze, "Mental Health Problems of Prison and Jail Inmates," U.S. Department of Justice, Bureau of Justice Statistics, Special Report (September 2006), www.bjs.gov/content/pub/pdf/mhppji.pdf.*

The good news is changes are being made. Many state and local government agencies have been exploring progressive, analytically oriented options for improving our justice system. Programs such as the National Association of Counties' Smart Justice[6] effort and the Bureau of Justice Assistance's Smart Policing Initiative[7] have increased the awareness of how to effectively utilize data and analytics to enable more evidence-based decisions.

In order for agencies and practitioners to be able to use analyzed data more effectively, they must first be able to access the information. The criminal justice and public safety sector looks very different than it did years ago. Today, almost every encounter with an offender or member of the public is captured electronically and leaves a digital footprint. The influx of data available to state and local agencies presents unique challenges to practitioners and policy makers. First, they need to effectively integrate data sets, with the appropriate permissions, so the right individuals have the necessary access to data. Governance and data-sharing initiatives are vital to this portion of the process. Second, the data needs to be of high quality and trusted for decision making. Finally, law enforcement and justice personnel need to be able to analyze the data and operationalize the results to help with life-altering decisions, often in real time.

## IMPROVING DATA ACCESS AND DATA QUALITY

Justice and public safety data resides in systems such as computer-aided dispatch (CAD), records management systems (RMS), criminal history, court, jail, intelligence, and dozens of other databases. The data sets are owned by law enforcement, criminal justice, corrections, homeland security, and other agencies. The information comes in many difference formats and includes both structured (fields) and unstructured (narratives) data. It is important to note that data sharing and interoperability are key initiatives following 9/11. However, agencies are still protective of their data and require safeguards to ensure that information is protected.

## Access to Data

As more data is captured, justice and public safety practitioners have greater access to data than ever before. However, to most effectively serve the public, they need even more access to data sets that they currently cannot easily utilize. Two key data sets that can provide additional valuable information are mental health data and social services data. Considering privacy regulations and concerns, portions of the data will need to be concealed to protect the individual. The data can be segmented and protected so that only certain information is shared based on user role and security. Pointer systems and flags can be provided to users to alert them to the presence of particular information without providing HIPPA-protected information. The goal should be to alert law enforcement about individuals who have mental health issues or are involved in social services programs. This information could help determine how officers interact with these individuals to ensure the best possible outcome.

Consider officers serving a warrant or approaching someone at a traffic stop. Wouldn't the officer want to know the criminal history, gun permit information, and outstanding warrants as well as mental health issues and involvement in treatment programs? This information will help them approach each situation with the appropriate level of caution, keeping the individual, the public, and the officers safer. Providing access to mental health and social service data would ensure that individuals who would benefit from treatment programs are provided those options. Law enforcement, court personnel, probation officers, and others can use the data to identify possible diversionary actions and alternatives to incarceration. The positive impacts of utilizing data early in the process could benefit the officers, the public, the offender, and the justice system as a whole.

## Data Preparation

As access to data is improved for law enforcement and criminal justice agencies, a parallel step is to prepare the data so it can be effectively utilized. The most important steps are integrating the data, improving the data quality, and performing entity resolution. Today's technology makes it possible to continually integrate disparate data sets from a wide variety of programs and systems. The information can then be provided, via a customized view, for each set of practitioners. Officers can receive updated offender information prior to making an initial approach or responding to a call for service. Court personnel can have accurate, real-time, cross-jurisdiction information to help determine if holding an individual is warranted. Probation officers can receive automated alerts if one of their probationers has an encounter with law enforcement.

As data access through integration is being achieved, steps need to be taken to enhance the data quality. This can be the difference between making a correct or incorrect decision. Data quality improvements such as deconflicting a name, date of birth, address, phone number, and so on can have a profound impact on decision making. Enhancing the quality and consistency of data enables criminal justice and law enforcement to fully understand each individual and make real-time decisions with the appropriate information.

## Entity Resolution

An additional step to improve data quality is to perform entity resolution. The ability to resolve the data and build a golden record of an offender is incredibly valuable as it allows practitioners to more effectively analyze the data. Coupling unique identifiers (name, DOB, SSN) and reviewing additional fields such as address, phone number, and associates can allow record-keepers to build toward a single record for an individual. Every time law enforcement data is improved, it gives analysts and detectives a better chance of identifying associations and patterns within the data that can help them improve public safety and solve crime.

Law enforcement and criminal justice agencies need to make integrating data, managing data, and improving data quality top organizational priorities. As more and more data is generated, it becomes challenging to identify actionable intelligence, key evidence, and requisite information that is buried in the data. The value could be realized at each step in the criminal justice process.

## North Carolina CJLEADS

In 2008, the state of North Carolina experienced a tragedy that made the legislature realize it needed a better way to provide criminal justice practitioners with relevant, real-time data. A homicide occurred after a case for an offender with probation violations that may have resulted in incarceration, was continued due to a clerical error. Without timely access to criminal history information from across the state, the offender was released and days later committed the homicide. As a result, the state decided it needed a comprehensive view of offenders from disparate justice systems that could be provided via a single user interface.

Like most states, North Carolina had criminal history data, court data, jail information, and other criminal justice data in dozens of silos throughout the state. They also had shrinking budgets, increased data volume, and constrained resources trying to identify information from their data. The state sought to provide a system to all criminal justice and law enforcement practitioners that would integrate, manage, cleanse, search, and analyze criminal justice information. They began by identifying key data sources. The state had to understand the limitations of their data including data-quality issues. They considered data-governance challenges and began putting in place memorandums of understanding to help address access and security issues. The goal was to reduce the time and effort associated with manual data searching and integration to prevent oversight of key pieces of data. Once access to important data sets enabled a comprehensive picture of an offender, they added watch list and alert capabilities to proactively monitor certain types of behavior. This functionality has saved the state millions of dollars per year in improved automation by reducing the amount of time justice and public safety practitioners spend searching for information.[8]

North Carolina has implemented a successful program where criminal justice and public safety data from multiple sources is integrated, deconflicted, and made available to practitioners on a daily basis. The result is a real-time, holistic view of an offender that is available to users of the system via multiple platforms. Danny Bell, the director of the North Carolina CJLEADS program, states that "CJLEADS is a tool to support criminal justice professionals with making quicker and more effective decisions. CJLEADS brings together disparate criminal justice data to help create a more rounded profile of offenders and provides a single source of information from a variety of criminal justice organizations—including court, warrant, probation, parole, and local jail information—which agencies can access securely via the web." Providing this type of access to criminal justice practitioners can result in improved efficiency and an increase in public safety. Since North Carolina implemented CJLEADS, more states have realized that timely access of accurate data is critical to making the correct decision. Applying analyzed, historical data to criminal justice decisions can improve the process even further.

## ANALYTICS THROUGHOUT THE JUSTICE AND PUBLIC SAFETY SYSTEM

Across the spectrum of the public safety community, analyzed data can enable decision making to help stop the cycle of people revolving through the system. Analytics can assist in identifying who will be better served by alternative, evidence-based options. Risk-assessment models can inform decision making about what level of intervention is appropriate. Investigations can be streamlined by linking individuals and events across disparate datasets. The opportunities are limitless.

### Analytics in Juvenile Justice

Let's first discuss how the use of analyzed data can be applied during the juvenile justice process. If we can avoid having nonviolent young offenders enter the justice system, and reduce the cycle of recidivism, it can have a positive impact on each individual, their family, and the future justice system. To do so, juvenile justice personnel need analyzed data to help them answer the following questions. What are the risks and needs facing this individual? What options are available that would provide the most positive outcome for young offenders? What programs are most effective? Agencies need to utilize their past experiences and leverage analytics tools to help case workers do what is best for each youth based on their unique circumstances. The

Oregon Youth Authority (OYA) is a great example of how analytics can inform the entire spectrum of decision making within the juvenile justice system.

## Oregon Youth Authority

In 2013, the OYA deployed an initiative called the Youth Reformation System to help their personnel make decisions based on analyzed, historical data. The focus of the program was to improve the agency's population forecast, placement and treatment decisions, and program evaluation. The system uses a wide range of analytic tools to gain a comprehensive view of each youth. For example, there are tools that predict the likelihood of a repeat offense and another that provide clarity into the child's personality and attributes. A third tool combines this information and provides predictive analysis of how the youth might respond to different programs and environments.

The OYA established a process where each incoming youth offender was evaluated and a recidivism risk was calculated. The assessment measured variables that impact recidivism including prior weapons offense referrals, misdemeanor referrals, felony referrals, and other variables. This information was combined with a set of research-based typologies to help characterize each youth. Factors including school performance, relationships, family structure, and historical drug use help the OYA get a clearer understanding of each young offender. The combination of this information enables juvenile justice personnel to make the most informed, fact-based decision at each decision point for every individual.

The OYA had collected years of information related to each youth, their environment, their offenses, and the programs to which they were assigned. This enabled the OYA to prove the value of making analytically driven decisions; in this case, around placement. One example shared by Paul Bellatty, OYA's research manager, was that by "analyzing past cases, we found that the recidivism rate of youth who were in the wrong placement was 36 percent, versus 21 percent for those who were in the best placement option [as defined by the tool]."

In addition to the use of analyzed data, there are other technology advances that can assist juvenile justice stakeholders. Agencies can now take advantage of watch list capabilities that can alert case workers should a youth be involved in an interaction with law enforcement. This automation can be implemented to help get young offenders the help they need, as quickly as possible. The result is a reduction in the likelihood that a child will have multiple incidents that lead to a pattern of criminal activity. While the OYA programs and watch list functionality focuses on the juvenile justice population, similar analytic programs can be implemented throughout criminal justice agencies.

## Analytics in Adult Offender System

The adult offender system can leverage historical data and analytical approaches as well. In addition to the use cases described earlier, pretrial decisions can benefit from a comprehensive understanding of an offender's circumstances. What is the best option to keep the person from offending again? What are the social and economic impacts of each decision? For example, a person is charged with narcotics possession and a decision had to be made regarding bond. Criminal history, family, social services received, education, health, living environment, and other factors should be analyzed when making the decision. Perhaps the best decision is not to hold the person on bond due to the impact to the individual and their family. If the person cannot afford bond and loses their job as a result, there is a negative impact on their family and perhaps a higher likelihood of remaining in the system. Court personnel have years of data available to them that can be analyzed and applied so that the best possible future decisions can be made.

Sometimes incarceration is the best option. If the decision is leaning toward detention, are there alternatives to state prison and jail time that could have a positive effect on the offender? Home confinement, electronic monitoring, community corrections centers, probation, and other methods are options for individuals charged with nonviolent crimes that can help ease the burden on the prison system. Analytics combined with a comprehensive view of an offender will allow practitioners to make more informed, fact-based decisions to help each individual offender.

The same exercise can be conducted when determining treatment options available to an offender convicted of a particular crime.

Considering the individual's critical factors (criminal history, education, family, etc.), what incarceration and treatment programs, based on analysis of historical data, present the best option for the individual? Perhaps detention coupled with involvement in vocational and social service support programs has proven to be the most effective path for certain offenders. Predictive modeling can be applied to the data to identify inmates who have a lower risk of recidivism and who could benefit from a noncustodial sentence. Practitioners can optimize incarceration and rehabilitation programs by using analytics to identify which offenders will likely receive the most benefit from these alternative programs.

## Florida Department of Corrections

The State of Florida Department of Corrections (Florida DOC) successfully uses analytics to protect the public and rehabilitate offenders. Florida DOC integrated dozens of data sources and made the data available for reporting and analysis. Their staff had been inundated with requests from various stakeholders for annual, monthly, and weekly reports in addition to ad hoc reports about specific inmate populations. One of the challenges they faced was how to best allocate scarce program resources. Florida DOC uses analyzed data to identify inmates with specific needs or risk of recidivism and ensure they receive priority ranking for program interventions proven to provide the best outcomes. The model predicts inmate recidivism and ensures those who would most benefit from program intervention are assigned to the program. David Ensley, research director for the Florida DOC, has stated that through analytics "we have the right information to deliver to our stakeholders, allocate our resources more efficiently, and preserve citizen safety."

If law enforcement and justice personnel can get more people the help they need earlier in the process, it can have a tangible impact on the number of people involved in the criminal justice system. We can reduce the number of incarcerated individuals and re-allocate the costs associated with prisons and jails to social services and treatment programs. Analytics can also be used throughout the prisons and jails to determine which programs and which treatment paths resulted in the highest success. By utilizing data-driven decisions, we can increase the chances for success for each individual and have a profound impact on the prison system and society as a whole.

## Analytics in Investigations

Traditional law enforcement activities provide another area where analyzed data can be applied to improve processes. Preventing crimes, conducting investigations, and building cases provide another use case for analytics. Law enforcement has greater volumes of data available to them than ever before. Today, investigators and analysts manually review and piece together information to identify actionable intelligence. Through interviews, surveillance, and information from informants, officers work to create lists of potential suspects and build a case worthy of charges. Too much time is spent searching for key information and connections. Performing seemingly simple searches and analysis can be challenging against existing public safety systems. For instance, most public safety systems can search field data within their system, but cannot search and analyze the notes, narratives, and attachments. These nonstructured sources of data house key information vital for investigators to identify actionable intelligence.

Law enforcement must use data and analytics tools to help them identify key starting points of an investigation and focus their time on building their case. For instance, analytics can search through structured and unstructured data throughout multiple databases to identify key intelligence an analyst may never find. Analytic tools can be used to identify social networks based on people, places, phone numbers, evidence, etc. If an analyst can more effectively identify that multiple suspects are connected via other common factors, law enforcement can prioritize investigative activities and more effectively build cases. Going back to the discussion about access to data, this type of analysis is most beneficial when investigators have access to nontraditional law enforcement data. Examples including hunting and fishing license data, social services data, select medical information, and mental health data can help conduct investigations.

Investigators also spend a disproportionate amount of time reviewing financial information trying to follow the money in narcotics, cyber-crimes, and human trafficking cases. Officers need the ability to run financial analysis of a suspect's income and other data. Often times, large sums of cash are found at a suspect's home and detectives need to determine if that money was attained via illegal activities. Today, investigators utilize manual processes to track money or to determine how suspects launder money gained from illegal activities. They analyze cash transactional reports to understand how often suspects make large deposits and where the money is deposited. All of these activities are key to building a case when narcotics, cyber-crime, and human trafficking are the motive and law enforcement needs to utilize technology to keep up with the criminals.

Social media is a relatively new and constantly growing source of key data that may be available to law enforcement. Facebook, Twitter, Instagram, and Snapchat are just a few of the dozens of social media sites that house information vital to successful resolution of investigations. We sometimes see incidents of violence where a review of the suspects' social media profiles reveals clues that could have been valuable to law enforcement. Text analytics tools can help identify behaviors that cause law enforcement to conduct interviews or surveillance. Of course, access to social media data would need to be in compliance with the provider's terms. With the amount of data that is available today, no one can effectively review social media data manually. Instead organizations need to leverage technology to identify actionable intelligence, provide alerts, and then deploy traditional law enforcement activities to disrupt violent attacks.

## CONCLUSION

The goal of this chapter has been to illustrate how access to data and the use of analyzed data can provide criminal justice and public safety personnel with the means to better perform their jobs. As you have read in prior sections, justice and public safety touches almost all facets of state and local government. Departments tasked with improving education, child well-being, decreasing prescription drug abuse, fighting fraud, and others all have ties to our criminal justice agencies. Providing practitioners with robust data and timely analysis can enable them to make decisions that can improve the current and future health and effectiveness of all levels of the criminal justice and public safety system.

**PROFILE**

**David Kennedy,** as senior industry consultant at SAS Institute, helps criminal justice and public safety agencies utilize data to identify actionable intelligence and implement analytics throughout their organization. He received his BBA from the University of Miami and an MBA from Nova Southeastern University.

## NOTES

1. Roy Walmsley, "World Prison Population List, tenth edition," International Centre for Prison Studies, University of Essex (October 2013), www.apcca.org/uploads/10th_Edition_2013.pdf.

2. Christian Henrichson and Ruth Delaney, "The Price of Prisons, What Incarceration Costs Taxpayers," Vera Institute of Justice (July 2012), http://archive.vera.org/sites/default/files/resources/downloads/price-of-prisons-updated-version-021914.pdf.

3. Doris J. James and Lauren E. Glaze, "Mental Health Problems of Prison and Jail Inmates," U.S. Department of Justice (September 2006), www.bjs.gov/content/pub/pdf/mhppji.pdf.

4. Henrichson and Delaney, "The Price of Prisons."

5. James Bonta, "The Effect of Prison on Criminal Behaviour," Solicitor General Canada (November 1999), https://www.publicsafety.gc.ca/cnt/rsrcs/pblctns/ffct-prsn/ffct-prsn-eng.pdf.

6. "Smart Justice," National Association of Counties, www.naco.org/resources/programs-and-initiatives/smart-justice.

7. Edmund McGarrell and Julie Wartell, "Smart Policing Initiative (SPI)," Bureau of Justice Assistance, U.S. Department of Justice, www.bja.gov/ProgramDetails.aspx?Program_ID=80.

8. David T. McCoy, "North Carolina Government Data Analytics Center Program," North Carolina Office of the State Controller (February 2014), https://ncit.s3.amazonaws.com/s3fs-public/documents/files/GDAC-Legislative-Report-February-2014.pdf.

# CHAPTER 7

# Brilliant Analytics for Smart Cities

*Jennifer Robinson*

Our nation is changing. Our world is changing. Our agrarian society is moving into urban apartments and suburban townhomes, causing the populations of our cities to swell and the populations of our rural counties to shrink. Globally, 54 percent of the world's population lives in urban areas today. By 2045, the number of people living in cities worldwide will increase by 1.5 times to 6 billion.[1] The U.S. Census in 2010 reported that 80.7 percent of Americans live in either towns or cities.[2]

Immigration is also on the rise as people are moving in greater numbers than ever before. Roughly 42 million people immigrated into the United States in 2014. With immigrants making up 13.3 percent of our country's citizenry—the highest percentage since 1919—our country is seeing an increase in ethnic diversity.[3] The effect of this immigration is reflected in the U.S. Census Bureau prediction that by 2045, no one race will be in the majority in the United States.[4]

And, the values of people are changing. A new generation of workers is coming into the workforce with different priorities. Millennials seek work–life balance and place a higher value on careers that are performed for a worthy purpose.[5] The Deloitte 2016 Millennial study found that millennials place work–life balance above career progression.[6] In addition, people are showing a preference for spending their money on meaningful experiences rather than acquiring objects. According to the Elite Daily Millennial Consumer Study of 2015, millennials are also socially and civically aware and engaged, in part due to their connectivity through the Internet and cell phones. In fact, 87 percent of millennials reported using between two and three tech devices at least once on a daily basis.[7] And, as people place a greater importance on virtual mobility than physical mobility, the average person's daily use of his car has shrunk to almost a fourth of the amount of time he uses his cell phone.[8] So, it is not surprising that the number of people getting their driver's license is going down. The cell phone has another important impact: immediacy. With cell phones readily providing quick answers and easy solutions, people expect immediate answers to more questions than their predecessors ever dreamed of asking.

As our societies morph, technology is also morphing and advancing at a rapid clip. Significant advances in telecommunication technology have fostered unprecedented connectedness. Approximately 84.2 percent of

Americans are connected to the Internet[9] that provides a portal for socializing, recreating, shopping, learning, and working. The number of smartphone users in the United States continues to rise with approximately 207,200,000 smart phones in use today.[10] Everyday living now relies on information technology.

The needs, lifestyle, and demands of a changing population and the lingering effects of the Great Recession are impacting the finances of local governments. Some cities have experienced decreased revenue growth per capita. Because people are buying smaller or less expensive homes and because businesses are no longer providing private offices for every employee, capital investment (and, consequently, revenue) is not keeping pace with the population growth. Other local governments have experienced worse: no revenue growth. Some counties and small cities are no longer attracting new investment as people are packing their bags and moving to the big city.

In my role as an elected official of a medium-sized municipality, I can see how these demographic and societal changes are coming together to impact how local governments serve their citizens. With changing populations, higher expectations for services, and fewer dollars, we find ourselves in a position of trying to do more with less.

But, most cities have one resource in abundance: data. Like unmined gold in the rocks below City Hall, data can be very lucrative for a city. Mining data provides a wealth of information that can be used to cut expenses, improve efficiencies, and make an organization more effective. In other words, using data strategically can compensate for the limited financial and human resources with which we are working as we strive to meet the higher expectations of our citizens.

The most important thing I have to tell you is this: using data is critical for local governments—so critical that its importance puts its use at the center of the smart city solutions that are being implemented in local governments across the globe.

## SMART CITIES

The term *smart city* has become an umbrella term that encapsulates a movement among governments to use new technologies. The technologies being used vary widely, which has led to some confusion about what a smart city is and what a government must do to be considered smart. But, at the core, I believe that most definitions of a smart city boil down to this: a smart city solution is one in which a local government uses information technology to improve the lives of its citizens.

Any local government can earn the title of smart city. The word *city* suggests that the smart city movement only applies to cities. However, any town, borough, county, quasi-governmental agency, or local authority can employ technologies that make them a smart city.

Because many smart city initiatives have begun in large cities with highly publicized grants and results, many people believe that only larger governments can embark on smart city solutions. However, governments of any size can use new technologies. In fact, small to medium, high-growth communities may be best positioned for applying smart city solutions. With less infrastructure to retrofit, increased revenue from new development, financial participation from stakeholders, and a dynamic citizenry, a growing city is often most nimble when it comes to revamping its technology and operations.

With the implementation of technology, one size does not fit all. The technology needs for local governments vary widely because governments differ greatly from each other. Local governments are unique from one another based on how they are created, their local authorities and responsibilities, the laws they impose upon themselves, their geography and demographics, and the distinct nature of their home-grown operations.

There are over 19,000 municipalities across the United States. They vary in size, with New York City being the largest megacity at roughly 8 million people, and Buford, Wyoming with only one resident. Most cities across America are small to medium in population with a surprisingly few number of cities—only about 300 across the nation—with populations of 100,000 or more people.

Municipalities typically derive their identity, role, responsibilities, and authorities from the legislature of their state and in response to the unique needs of its citizens. In states with Home Rule, a municipality has the authority to impose regulations, expend funds, and provide services in any manner unless expressly prohibited by the state. In contrast, in states that follow Dillon's Rule, municipalities only have the authority expressly given to it by the state. This rule is sometimes referred to as Mother May I, since municipalities must ask for permission to pass ordinances, levy taxes, or provide infrastructure and services.

While state law influences whether a city or county operates schools, runs utilities such as water and sewer or electricity, and provides social services, the values and demands of its citizens further shape what a government does. Adjacent cities with similar authorities can be very different from one another as they develop infrastructure, operations, and laws in response to what their citizens want. While my municipality provides hourly water meter readings to its citizens via a web portal, our neighboring towns manually read meters and report usage on a monthly basis. Likewise, one county may address the homelessness problem with temporary shelters while another addresses homelessness with permanent housing programs.

Most cities operate under one of two forms of government: mayor–council (often referred to as strong mayor) or council–manager. In a mayor–council city, the citizens elect the mayor who works as the manager of the city, overseeing its operations. In a council–manager city, the citizens elect the mayor and council who hire and direct a manager. The manager oversees the operations of the city. The form of government under which a city is established often influences the implementation of technology in a city. A visionary mayor can spur its community to embrace new technologies. In contrast, a stable manager-led organization can provide longevity to an initiative that might have otherwise been disbanded by a change of strong mayors.

Regardless of the different authorities, responsibilities, or organization of each local government, all strive to run as effectively and efficiently as possible for the benefit of their taxpayers, employees, and customers. Our perennial quest for improvement is now aided by emerging technologies.

## TECHNOLOGIES IN SMART CITY SOLUTIONS

Emerging technologies such as the Internet of things (IoT), telecommunications, social media, cloud-based computing and data storage, and analytics enable city officials to meet their specific goals and address their unique challenges. The use of these different technologies falls under the smart city umbrella. Many smart city solutions involve a combination of these technologies.

## IoT and Telecommunications

The Internet has revolutionized the way we live, work, and communicate. In addition to connecting humans, the Internet is now connecting objects and allowing them to communicate with one another. To enable this communication through the Internet, software is now embedded in all types of everyday objects. Even streetlights, which were previously inert and non-communicative, can contain electronics, software, sensors, and network connectivity.

Sensors and meters empower the streetlights to collect data on elements such as traffic, weather, the presence of humans, or the need for emergency services. Telecommunications allows the data that is collected by the streetlights' sensors and meters to be sent to central databases for near-instant analysis. The vast network of objects that collect and communicate information—such as meters, sensors, cell phones, vehicles, buildings, and machinery—is referred to as the Internet of Things (IoT).

## IoT

Connected objects can be accessed, metered, and controlled remotely through an organization's network infrastructure, as well as directly integrated with the computer-based systems that governments use to manage business and run operations. As we strive to provide the greatest level of service and the best infrastructure for the least amount of expense, IoT can play a vital role in helping to achieve our goals. For example, cities are using sensors at intersections to monitor congestion and communicate via software that adjusts signals in real time to reduce congestion. Automated meters gather water and electricity consumption information and send it to databases at regular, frequent intervals for analysis, enabling cities to understand and influence utility consumption. And, location data collected from cellphones is enlightening city planners about the typical movements of their citizens in, out, and around the city.

The number of connected objects is expected to grow to approximately 20.8 billion by 2020.[11] These connected objects will produce approximately 10 percent of the anticipated 44 zettabytes of data stored in 2020.[12]

## Social Media

Just as connected objects, devices, and machines are collecting copious amounts of new and useful data, people are also generating data. For example, people freely provide information about themselves to companies through their inquiries and purchases on the Internet—information that can be analyzed to gain insights about them. Similarly, as people share their thoughts, preferences, dislikes, and concerns on social media, those personal sentiments become data, which can be collected, retained, and analyzed by cities to understand trends, identify issues, monitor sentiments, and make better decisions.

## Cloud-Based Computing and Data Storage

Because our organizations are collecting data at a faster rate than ever before, we are creating and accumulating massive volumes of data that must be securely stored, managed, and accessed. Governments can store their vast collection of data in offsite, Internet-accessible storage, referred to as the cloud. This storage is secure and scalable. Because the local governments are essentially renting data storage when using cloud storage, we can use our operating budget to pay for it, rather than spending capital budgets to buy equipment.

One of the biggest benefits of cloud-based storage is the flexibility it provides regarding storage and computational power, as both can scale on demand to meet an organization's needs. Our organizations no longer need to buy more space or processing capability than needed, nor are we at risk of running out of space or running slower due to inadequate space or processing capacity. In addition, using cloud-based storage reduces the cost and hassle of maintaining and running servers and databases; cloud-hosting companies take care of database maintenance, backups, security, and data movements for their customers.

While IoT, telecommunications, social media, and cloud-based storage are valuable technologies that can be used in smart city solutions, governments can actually implement a smart city solution without them. Consider the fact that the software systems used by various local government departments generate most of our organizations' data. Data management and analytics alone can provide incredible value by combining data from many disparate systems and databases in order to reveal findings that help individual departments use their data better. For example, a city is smart when it combines its police and code enforcement data to better understand the relationship between crime and property neglect.

Regardless of how a jurisdiction's information is collected, communicated, or stored, smart city solutions always share three characteristics: data is collected, analyzed, and leveraged to improve the organization's services or infrastructure. The essential element is analytics—because without it, the true value of IoT cannot be realized, the breadth of information produced by social media cannot be tapped, and an organization's operational and infrastructure data cannot be fully used to identify opportunities for improvements and efficiencies.

## DATA MANAGEMENT

Leveraging these technological advancements creates a new set of challenges—particularly around data's explosive growth and its management. According to the International Data Corporation (IDC), the amount of data created doubles every two years.[13] Cities are contributing to this trend, generating vast amounts of new data through technologies. If we manage, integrate, and harness this data effectively, we will be able to maximize our organizations' efficiencies and effectiveness.

Managing data can be a huge task for cities with software systems and databases in different departments at City Hall. To integrate and manage their data, some organizations embark on an initiative referred to as data governance, which includes a group of people tasked with overseeing the definition of a set of data procedures and a plan to execute those procedures. Within this initiative, data standards are defined and security rules are established so that data can be integrated.

A thorough integration will include scrubbing the data for accuracy by detecting and correcting or removing corrupt or inaccurate records from a record set, table, or database. This scrubbing is essential for the most important smart city technology: analytics.

## ANALYTICS

Once clean data is stored in databases, city governments can use sophisticated analytical software—which employs mathematics, statistics, modeling, and machine learning—to turn it into valuable information and insights. The algorithms used in analytics perform work in seconds that would take humans weeks to perform, such as sifting through incredibly large volumes of data, data that is recorded at a rapid clip, and unstructured data. Analytics empowers a local government to quickly identify correlations and trends. Furthermore, high-performance analytics software can process millions of events per second, making the previously insurmountable task of understanding data an achievable feat.

### Analytics for Large Volumes of Data

Local governments can use analytical software to process vast amounts of data and equip decision makers and service providers with the intelligence they need to make knowledge-based decisions. The application of advanced analytics to large volumes of data provides insight into what has happened, why something happened, and what future outcomes and trends may be. An organization can predict the impact of various actions or decisions, such as the result of locating a police substation in different parts of the city. Armed with insights from their data, government officials can make faster and more informed decisions.

Pinal County, Arizona is using analytics in the campaign to protect its public from dangerously high temperatures. Investigators treat heat stroke, hyperthermia, and heat shock like other epidemiological threats, such as food-borne illness or norovirus. They look for spikes and clusters among populations and within certain geographies.

Pinal County analyzed years of data from the statewide mortality databases and hospital discharge data to uncover patterns and risk factors for heat-related illness. The heat illness project required analytics to make sense of a million rows and 200 columns of data.

Investigators thought they would see more heat-related illness among the elderly. But analysis showed that younger people are most at risk. Graham Briggs, administrator for the Pinal County disease investigation program, credits analytics with identifying an unexpected at-risk population. With this knowledge, Pinal County is tailoring its outreach to provide citizens with information to protect themselves.

Briggs's team also identified clusters of heat-related illness in poorer parts of the county. They did so by integrating geospatial and socioeconomic data.

In addition to heat-related illnesses, Pinal County disease investigators monitor the spread of hundreds of infectious and sexually transmitted diseases. They conduct biosurveillance by using analytics to find anomalies in disease data.

"It's easy to spot something severe, like Hanta, meningitis, or Ebola," said Briggs. "For something like salmonella, it's more difficult. Cases trickle in. It may take weeks to identify a cause. Analytics spots the trend earlier and helps public health officials focus their investigation."

## Analytics for Data Received at a Rapid Clip

With the advent of IoT objects collecting and communicating information, analytics has advanced to be able to process information at a rapid rate. Not only can analytics software process millions of records in databases per second, but analytics software is now being located in the objects that collect the information.

When analytics software is applied to IoT, it's referred to as the Analytics of Things (AoT). AoT empowers devices and machines to run analytics at the source of data collection, which means that information no longer has to be transferred to a central database prior to analysis. Rather, data can be analyzed as it is created and then captured and delivered to a central database for further analysis and action. The result is real-time analytics that deliver insights within seconds of data being collected, allowing objects or people to take informed, immediate action. Because analysis occurs prior to the communication of information to a centralized database, collected data that doesn't have value may be purged. As a result, only valuable information is communicated to the centralized database, which reduces the cost of data transmission.

One of the primary virtues of connected analytics is that you can aggregate data from multiple devices and make comparisons across time and users that can lead to better decisions. A few examples of AoT capacity include:

- Understanding patterns and reasons for variation
- Detecting anomalies
- Predicting asset maintenance
- Optimizing processes
- Prescription (using data to direct employees' actions)
- Situational awareness

Analytics is often a precursor to informed action. VR Group, the railway in Finland, turned to the IoT and analytics to keep its fleet of 1,500 trains on the rails and provide a better, safer experience for its customers.

In constant operation in all kinds of weather, these trains endure harsh conditions. So it's no surprise that a large portion of VR Group's operational costs go toward maintenance. To reduce costs and maximize uptime, VR Group wanted to move from a traditional maintenance approach that focused on replacing parts as needed.

In recent years, VR Group began fitting sensors on various systems and subsystems to monitor symptoms of wear and other failures. But the sensors themselves only collect the raw data. The real benefit comes in analyzing that data, often in real time, to allow engineers to take faster, more appropriate responses.

Traditionally, VR Group approached maintenance in two ways. Major systems, like wheels and bogies, were covered by scheduled maintenance. Often, parts were replaced when they still had a lot of life left. The other method was to fix things, like doors, when they broke down. These were hard to forecast and could lead to missed routes and unhappy customers.

VR Group developed a predictive maintenance program that focuses on monitoring the condition of parts at all times. In this program, mathematical models predict when parts are likely to fail so that they can be replaced before they cause unplanned downtime. By looking at sensor data, analytics software gives VR Group a real-time overview of its fleet. The railway company's goal is to change its maintenance approach, so eventually everything will be based on real-time monitoring.

"If a door on a train starts to open and close slower than usual, it is likely to break down within a certain time frame, and we must do something before that happens," says Kimmo Soini, senior vice president for maintenance at VR Group. "Analytics allows us to develop our repair operations around predictive maintenance."

By looking at new and historical data, analytics software helps VR Group plan the maximum interval between certain maintenance events, like turning wheels (on a lathe) or replacing the wheel-and-axle sets on the trains. Each train has more than 30,000 of these sets. If VR Group can optimize the dates of turning, it can keep trains on the rails longer. "In fact, we might be able to reduce the amount of maintenance work by one third," says Soini.

Analytics also helps VR Group identify the root causes of failures, which can increase savings and improve the reliability of the trains. Additionally, effective insight into IoT enables the railway company to minimize stock levels of spare parts and materials, keeping only what it needs on hand.

"The amount of sensor data has grown extensively, and the controlling of the data has become more targeted. Sensor data, analytics— and the automation of the two—are the technological advances we need in order to take the next step," says Soini. "I believe that all maintenance will sooner or later be transformed by the Internet of Things, in all industries.

"VR Group's vision is to become the leading travel company in Finland. In my opinion, we could not make this happen without predictive analytics."

## Analytics for Unstructured Data

In the late 1960s, the Navy created something revolutionary in the computer industry: a computer system that searched the heading and text of messages destined for naval units afloat for flag words or phrases which they used to identify various aspects of the message. Flag words and phrases embedded in messages would prompt software to process the message in a particular way. It took decades for this technology to move to other forms of government and industries. Today, the computerized process of analyzing unstructured text to identify sentiments, trends, and business intelligence is known as text analytics or text mining.

Local governments are now able to glean valuable information from their citizens' emails and social media posts. Through the application of algorithms to text, governments put their unstructured data into meaningful context. While police departments are using the collection and study of text from social media to identify gang activity, their counterparts in the parks departments are using text analytics to assess the successes or weaknesses of festivals and programs.

The Alberta Environment and Parks system uses analytics to glean information from the satisfaction surveys that its customers complete. With approximately 250 campgrounds and 14,000 campsites that receive more than 1.8 million overnight visitors every year, Alberta Environment and Parks receives tens of thousands of completed surveys each year.

"Almost 80 percent of those people provided text-based data," says Roy Finzel, Manager of Business Integration and Analysis for Alberta Environment and Parks. "When you get that number of surveys returned, that's very significant."

In the past, an Alberta Environment and Parks analyst would spend three weeks at the end of the season inputting the text data, manually assigning a code to each comment. Now Alberta Environment and Parks uses analytics software that applies information retrieval and data-mining techniques across a variety of feedback channels—phone calls, email, surveys, and social media—with both structured and unstructured data. Instead of waiting for an end-of-season slide show, Alberta Environment and Parks' regional and district management get weekly feedback based on those text comments.

That feedback leads to midstream operational changes with an immediate impact on the customer experience, says Finzel. For example, analytics revealed that park visitors felt the coin-operated showers didn't last long enough to warrant the cost. In midseason, Alberta Environment and Parks adjusted the length of the shower based on those comments. Ironically, later surveys showed customers didn't expect a shower that long, and worried the department might be wasting water. The shower length was adjusted again. Alberta Environment and Parks can respond throughout the season to customer feedback about everything from the cost of firewood to the timing of caretaking operations.

"That's the dynamic of this," says Finzel. "That's what changes from an organizational or cultural perspective. We're becoming more responsive."

## Analytics for Complex Issues

Analytics is enabling governments to tackle incredibly complex problems. While analyzing data sometimes confirms what an organization knows, it often uncovers surprising findings. Unexpected correlations reveal opportunities to influence outcomes and effectively resolve issues.

Fraud can be a particularly complex crime to uncover. While it can occur in many ways, it is often identified in revenue-generating programs, programs in which state or federal money is passed through a local government, and software systems from which information is stolen.

Los Angeles County employed analytics to identify potential fraud, enhance investigations, and prevent improper payments in its Department of Public Social Services (DPSS) public assistance programs. The DPSS offers temporary financial assistance, employment services, free/low-cost health insurance, food benefits, and in-home supportive services for the elderly and disabled.

The county uses social-network analysis and analytics to predict which benefit recipients and service providers are most likely to engage in fraudulent activity and create potentially large fund losses. By identifying historical patterns of fraudulent activity, investigators can focus on cases with a higher probability of fraud. These improved process efficiencies mean fraud investigators have more time to review high-risk cases.

Since deploying its fraud system, Los Angeles County has significantly improved efficiencies, uncovered more fraud, and accelerated investigations. Approximately 10 to 15 cases per month are referred, with more than 40 percent being positive for fraud. This has not only helped the county recover funds and prevent fraudulent payouts, it has also curtailed large collusive fraud rings before they ever got organized and did real damage.

## Analytics for Transparency

Transparency in government is one concept about which both political parties can agree. While we may not be seeking transparency for the same reasons, both Republicans and Democrats value opening the public's business to citizens. Open data can yield important and new findings, open lines of understanding and conversation between the government and its citizens, and promote legitimacy.

While there are many benefits of opening data up for use by citizens, doing so must be done carefully as local governments store private and confidential information about their citizens. A city should ensure that the data sets that are open are clean and valid.

Analytic tools assist citizens by synthesizing data into valuable and digestible information. Using a visual analytics tool, the State of North Carolina opened its 2017 budget for citizen scrutiny. The state put its budget and expense data into a web application that allows citizens to drill down and examine the details of the budget.

## Implementing Analytics

With so much to be gained from using analytics, why are more governments not already doing so? Tight budgets, limited resources, and policy hurdles hinder the adoption of new technologies. But, I believe that the organizational structure of local governments might be one of the biggest hindrances of all.

Local governments are typically organized into silos. City and county departments operate in isolation from one another. It is clear why operational silos have developed when one considers the significant difference in the purpose of each local government department.

The police chief is concerned about reducing crime. The downtown manager wants to create a vibrant local economy. The inspections director is tasked with ensuring the construction and maintenance of safe buildings. What do any of these tasks have to do with each other? On the surface, one might say, nothing. But, the real answer is actually—everything.

As local governments have become reliant on software and hardware to operate, their silos have been perpetuated. Local governments have built technology silos that serve their individual departments. While department-specific software is reasonable and necessary, having department-specific data is not. When data is confined to one department for its exclusive use, the local government does not have the opportunity to maximize the use of that data.

Organizations can break down these silos by intentionally finding ways to share data. This can be accomplished by storing data in a centralized database or by federated access to data in its existing data stores. Doing so will empower the city to run analytics across the organization and will make more data available to more employees.

Once data is integrated, analytics can be run within departments as well as across departments. For example, a city combines its police and code enforcement data to further understand the relationship between crime and property neglect. By making the right investments to appropriately address public safety and code enforcement, the city will enhance the vibrancy of its downtown.

The integrated database and enterprise-wide analytics are the backbone that a city can implement to maximize the use of other technologies and their growing collection of data (see Figure 7.1).

So, as we consider the opportunities for cities through the use of IoT, the Internet, communications, and advanced analytics, the question is: How does a city best embark on using new technologies?

Dr. Sokwoo Rhee, associate director of the Cyber-Physical Systems Program at the National Institute of Standards and Technology, describes the value of using data in smart city solutions: "Collecting data through sensors is one thing; but once you collect it, you have to extract the real value—the real information—out of the data. I always say this: data itself is basically ones and zeros . . . there really is not a lot of value in that itself. The real value comes out when you analyze

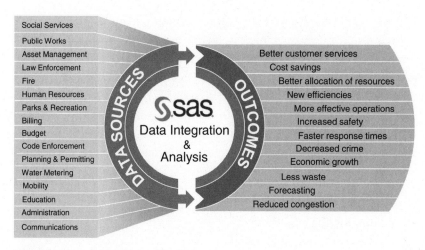

**Figure 7.1** Data Integration and Analysis
*Source: SAS Institute.*

the data to extract actionable information. This is probably one of the most important values created for smart cities."

With data being at the heart of smart city solutions, an integrated database with a strong analytics foundation is critical. Having an organized approach to storing and using data will allow a city to realize the maximum benefit of their smart city solutions. Creating a centralized data structure, sometimes referred to as a data analytics center, and embarking on using analytics requires several steps.

## Engage Leadership

Having a master plan for data integration and analytics is transformative for an organization. Therefore, the process begins with leadership. It is critical that the organization's governing body understands and believes in the long-term value of using analytics across the organization in order to optimize its services and infrastructure. In the short term, the governing body must also understand how each smart city solution will enhance the lives of its citizens.

## Identify the Business Problem

When approaching data integration and analytics, many governments find that the best approach is to *think big, but act small*. They begin by integrating only the datasets needed for their solution rather than embarking upon one huge integration effort for the entire organization. With this integration, they perform a discreet analytics solution that tackles one issue or process in the organization. This approach is more financially feasible, and it gently introduces leaders to the benefits of analytics. Once leaders see the return on investment from using analytics to address one issue, they are more open to applying analytics to solve other problems.

As a city considers which smart city solution to pursue, each solution should be evaluated on the basis of:

- The importance or criticality of the issue it resolves.
- The amount of data already collected around the issue.
- The cleanliness of that data.
- The return on investment of resolving the issue.

For cities with a goal of creating a data analytics center, this project becomes the cornerstone project of the framework.

### Survey Data

Cities often have more data stored than they are initially aware of. Before drafting a solution, staff should identify where data is stored and the quality of that data. How is the data generated? Is it entered by a person, automatically generated by a meter, collected from the Internet? In addition to the primary databases, staff should look for other databases that might store related information.

Most importantly, it is critical to have the appropriate data collected for a solution. For example, a forecasting model may only need 15 to 20 data points. A city may have so much data that these data points are easy to collect. Or, the city may not have collected all of the data it needs, in which case this revelation prompts the city to deliberately collect data.

Whether a city has too much data or too little data, analytics is valuable in helping a city become more effective in collecting and using its data.

### Determine the Best Approach

There are different ways in which a city may approach the implementation of an analytics solution. Cities may perform a results-as-a-service solution, a task-specific analytics solution, or an enterprise-wide approach.

In a results-as-a-service solution, the city poses a question it would like answered or a problem that it would like solved and provides the data to the analysts. The analysts integrate the data and run analytics to provide a one-time answer or solution.

For example, the Emergency Medical Services (EMS) of Wake County, NC wanted to know the optimum amount of time to deliver CPR to cardiac arrest patients for the best survival rates. Analysts collected and analyzed the organization's data and delivered an informed recommendation that was adopted by the EMS as its new practice.

A task-specific analytics solution is larger in scope than a results-as-a-service and may include a results-as-a-service project as one of its components.

In a task-specific analytics solution, the city provides access to its data for part of the organization in order to solve a specific problem or to perform a specific task. The analysts integrate the data and provide software that runs analytics on the data. While the data may either be stored on site in the city's offices or hosted by a third party, the city will take responsibility for using the software. New data will continue to be fed into the system that will run the analytics on an ongoing basis.

For example, the Town of Cary in North Carolina implemented an analytics tool to understand water consumption. Each hour, information from its customers' meters populates the database. Analysis is run on the collected data to determine incidents of anomalous consumption that alerts officials and citizens to potential leaks. The analyzed information is used for both billing and a customer information portal on which citizens can track their hourly, daily, weekly, and monthly consumption. Town officials use analytics not only to know how much water is being consumed, but to predict how future factors such as growth and weather events influence consumption and can determine the optimal timing of a plant expansion. A city may perform task-specific projects such as this one as a component of an enterprise-wide approach.

An enterprise-wide approach provides centrally managed access to data, through federation or a central repository, enabling a wide-ranging application of analytics. When a city adopts an enterprise-wide approach, it intends to manage its data across its departments and run analytics in and across its departments. A city typically undertakes an enterprise-wide approach in phases by performing several task-specific projects that establish the sharing of data and the growing use of analytics. Over time, the city continues to integrate data sources and enlarges the reach of the analytics tool. A city is ready for this approach when it dedicates resources such as a staff of data analysts or funds to hire a third-party analytics team to assist its employees in using analytics to solve problems or perform tasks.

### Perform Data Integration

The majority of analytical work lies in the preparation of the data. The many software systems that cities use collect information by different names and with different conventions. The pieces of data collected by the different systems are referred to as data elements. The object, person, place, event, or occurrence about which data is collected is considered the entity.

For example, a citizen is an entity in your database and her name and social security number are both data elements that describe her. When integrating data from different sources such as different departments' databases, the data elements must be consistent in order to build a clean record for the entity.

A police database may have a citizen identified by her full name, Kathryn Grace Johnson. However, that same citizen may be listed in the public works database by her customer number that is tied to her maiden name, Kathryn Wallace, and the parks department has her under her nickname, Katie Johnson. Before analysis can be run, the data needs to be combined and its elements must be reconciled.

Data management is the most laborious and time-consuming aspect of a data-analysis project; as the old term goes, garbage in, garbage out. To have comprehensive and defensible findings, the analytics must use good-quality, clean data.

### Employ Analytics

Depending on the approach the city takes, the analytics solution will be delivered in different ways. It may be a one-time answer to a question (as in a results-as-a-service solution) or it may be software that is provided to the city to use. Some analytics solutions will be tailored to specific tasks or issues with reports prepared for the city to use. Other solutions may be a software program that allows a city to analyze its data by applying quality-tested algorithms in order to get accurate and reliable answers.

Once a city has begun to use its analytics tool, its staff and elected leaders can adjust its operations and decision making according to their newly gleaned findings. And, staff and elected leaders can evaluate the benefit to the community. Very often, the results derived from one solution will inspire the city to embark on using analytics to solve other problems within the organization.

After Alberta Environment and Parks began seeing success with its surveys, it embarked on the implementation of content categorization and sentiment-analysis tools, with a particular eye to mining social media content. But the tools are not the be all and end all, says Finzel. There has to be a cultural commitment to applying the results operationally and strategically.

"It's been an evolutionary change in the way we do business, in terms of processing this kind of information and drawing insight from it, and the response of our management team," Finzel says.

Alberta Environment and Parks witnessed its own evolution in its use of analytics. Similarly, governments across the world are evolving in their awareness of smart city initiatives and the value of analytics. Government leaders are recognizing that their organizations can and should embark on using analytics.

Analytics is an exciting, new frontier for the business of running a local government. Our employees, taxpayers, and customers will all benefit tremendously as we put our valuable data to work.

---

**PROFILE**

**Jennifer Robinson** is director of local government solutions at SAS Institute. She helps cities and counties use analytics to be more efficient and serve their citizens more effectively. Robinson has served as a councilwoman for Cary, North Carolina, since 1999.

## NOTES

1. "Urban Development—Overview," The World Bank (October 10, 2016), www .worldbank.org/en/topic/urbandevelopment/overview.

2. "How many people reside in urban or rural areas for the 2010 Census? What percentage of the U.S. population is urban or rural?" United States Census Bureau, https://ask.census.gov/faq.php?id=5000&faqId=5971.

3. Migration Policy Institute, "U.S. Immigrant Population and Share over Time, 1850–Present," www.migrationpolicy.org/programs/data-hub/charts/immigrant -population-over-time.

4. Sarah Jo Peterson, "American Demography 2030: Bursting with Diversity, yet a Baby Bust," Urban Land Institute (January 15, 2015), http://urbanland.uli.org/ industry-sectors/american-demography-bursting-diversity-yet-baby-bust/.

5. "The 2016 Deloitte Millennial Survey: Winning Over the Next Generation of Lead-ers," Deloitte (2016), www2.deloitte.com/content/dam/Deloitte/global/Documents/ About-Deloitte/gx-millenial-survey-2016-exec-summary.pdf.

6. Ibid.

7. Elite Daily Staff, "Elite Daily Millennial Consumer Study 2015," Elite Daily.com, http://elitedaily.com/news/business/elite-daily-millennial-consumer-survey -2015/902145/.

8. Donald C. Shoup, "Cruising for Parking," *Transport Policy* 13 (July 24, 2006): 479–486, http://shoup.bol.ucla.edu/Cruising.pdf.

9. Internet Society, "Global Internet Penetration," InternetSociety.org, www .internetsociety.org/map/global-internet-report/?gclid=Cj0KEQjwmri_ BRCZpaHkuIH75_IBEiQAIG0rIaH1dKY36oisnZlPWrBhq1ULudq0Tku_ NHwsv7ZagiYaArFQ8P8HAQ.

10. Statista DMO, "Number of Smartphone Users in the United States from 2010 to 2021 (in millions)," Statista.com, https://www.statista.com/statistics/201182/forecast-of -smartphone-users-in-the-us/.

11. Gartner, "Gartner Says 6.4 Billion Connected 'Things' Will Be in Use in 2016, Up 30 Percent from 2015." Gartner.com (November 10, 2015), www.gartner.com/ newsroom/id/3165317.

12. "The Digital Universe of Opportunities: Rich Data and the Increasing Value of the Internet of Things—Executive Summary," EMC Digital Universe (April 2014), www.emc.com/leadership/digital-universe/2014iview/executive-summary.htm.

13. Ibid.

# CHAPTER 8

# Transportation

*Jim Trogdon*

The U.S. transportation system is a significant economic engine within our nation. It serves nearly 319 million citizens and 7.5 million businesses through a network of more than 4 million miles of roads, more than 19,000 public and private airports, and nearly 140,000 miles of railroads.[1] The value of U.S. transportation assets in 2014 was estimated at $7.7 trillion dollars, and the transportation sector accounts for $1.4 trillion or 8.6 percent of U.S. gross domestic product and 12.3 million jobs or 8.8 percent of the U.S. labor force.[2]

During the last two centuries the United States built this world-class transportation system that supported vast economic growth; however, as the system ages and demand grows we are falling behind. As stated by USDOT Secretary Anthony Foxx, "In the last century, we took over building the Panama Canal, completed the Interstate Highway System, and set the world standard in freight transport and aviation. But our lead has slipped away. We are behind—way behind. The quality of our roads, for example is no longer rated number 1, we are currently number 16."[3]

Fortunately, we have options. Technology and innovation has the potential to transform our transportation system and our personal mobility to an extent not seen since Henry Ford developed affordable automobiles for the masses and moved us from horseback to the automobile. Autonomous and connected vehicles have the potential to substantially transform personal mobility while generating vast quantities of data to significantly improve safety, improve transportation network performance, reduce congestion, and improve our quality of life. These new sources of data provide an opportunity to improve the efficiency of our transportation system while providing new mobility services and optimizing our transportation investments.

## CONNECTED AND AUTONOMOUS VEHICLES (CAVs)

A fully autonomous vehicle does not require a human driver but is fully operated by automation—they are computer driven using on-board sensing and three-dimensional, 360-degree mapping enabling the automation of all driving functions. High resolution 3-D mapping is the core technology that allows the potential for full automation.

A vehicle may not be fully autonomous but still have some autonomous, or automated features. The SAE International[4] defines six levels of automation depending on the level of human–driver interaction required. At Level 0, the human driver does everything, progressing through various reduced levels of human driver interaction that culminate at Level 5, where the automated system can perform all driving tasks, under all conditions that a human driver could perform them.

Conversely, connected vehicles use wireless technology to communicate with each other and to infrastructure. Connected vehicles may perform self-driving functions under certain conditions depending on their level of automation and on-board sensors. However, they are designed to share information wirelessly between vehicles to *assist* drivers. Connected vehicles utilize dedicated short-range communication (DSRC) 5.9 GHz and cellular technology to perform vehicle-to-vehicle (V2V) and vehicle-to-infrastructure (V2I) high-speed, low-latency broadcast communications (See Figure 8.1).

DSRC allows vehicles to broadcast a basic safety message every tenth of a second. The basic safety message includes information like position, heading, vehicle characteristics, and size. DSRC will allow a host of connected applications.

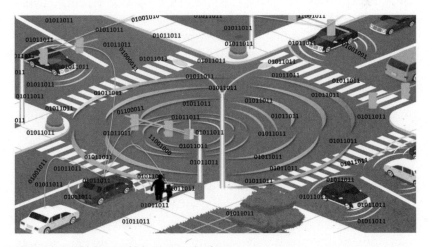

**Figure 8.1** Vehicle-to-Vehicle Communications
*Source: https://www.fhwa.dot.gov/publications/transopsupdate/15apr/index.cfm.*

## THE ROLE OF DATA AND ANALYTICS

A single connected or autonomous vehicle may broadcast up to 30 gigabytes of data per minute and collect more than 30 terabytes of data per day. As the transportation industry improves its capability in operational data capture from sensors, mobile devices, and connected vehicles, unprecedented amounts of data will be available. Imagine the opportunities to use real-time data from these sources and vehicles to improve safety and mobility. Complex analytical models can run on-board vehicles, within traffic sensors and signal controllers, and within cloud storage. Today, analysis of this type of data, where it exists, is post-storage and lags real time. With V2V and V2I capabilities, analysis can occur in real time by bringing the analytics to the data, instead of the data to the analytics. As this real-time data streams from one vehicle to another, onboard systems can determine if a vehicle crash has occurred beyond the line of sight or if the vehicle speed should be reduced in order to maximize green time at an upcoming series of traffic signals. Using streaming analytics you can spot meaningful trends, patterns, and correlations without transmitting all the data, and run complex analytical models for predictive and prescriptive decision outcomes. Streaming analytics is able to forecast expected values just a few seconds into the future, and compare actual to forecast to identify meaningful deviations to drive alerts or decisions. This type of analytics makes it possible to perform vehicle platooning, where multiple vehicles can travel at highway speeds while reducing the vehicle gap to less than a few feet. All vehicles in the platoon are operating and communicating with the lead vehicle. This allows for savings in fuel economy, reduced congestion, and improved safety.

While the same errors are repeated daily by human drivers, automation, analytics, and machine learning could allow for all autonomous and connected vehicles to learn from the experience of all other vehicles. Google clearly explains the benefits of its fully autonomous technology in one of its recent monthly reports.[5] "On the road, our car performs thousands of hardware and software checks every second to ensure that key components are working as intended. Because we're constantly monitoring our system, our cars are designed to detect an issue and determine whether it's small enough to continue driving (e.g., the tire pressure is low) or big enough to stop or pull over (e.g., a laser stops working). We employ complementary sensors and software, so our car doesn't rely on a single type of data to drive. For example, our suite of cameras, lasers, and radars work together to give our cars 360-degree visibility, so even if there's a glitch in one camera, our cars can still safely pull over. Likewise, our software uses a combination of algorithms that complement each other, so our cars don't rely on a single technique to detect others on the road and navigate safely. For critical driving functions, we go a step further and build in fully redundant systems. Arguably the most critical function in any kind of car is the driver. In today's cars, a backup human can't be installed to immediately take over if the driver is tired or distracted (despite the best efforts of backseat drivers!). In contrast, each of our self-driving vehicles is equipped with a secondary computer to act as a backup in the rare event that the primary computer goes offline. Its sole responsibility is to monitor the main computer and, if needed, safely pull over or come to a complete stop. It can even account for things like not stopping in the middle of an intersection where it could cause a hazard to other drivers. With layers of safety and redundant systems, we can develop a fully self-driving car that doesn't need to rely on a human as backup if something goes wrong. Given that human error and distracted driving are involved in 94 percent of crashes, this technology has the potential to make our roads dramatically safer."

## BENEFITS OF CONNECTED AND AUTONOMOUS VEHICLES

The benefits from CAVs are numerous. In 2015 alone, 35,092 people died on U.S. roadways. With an estimated 94 percent of all crashes tied to human error, there is a potential to substantially reduce fatal crashes and severe injuries through the implementation of this technology.[6] The National Highway and Transportation Safety Administration (NHTSA) estimates that just two of the connected vehicle safety applications, left turn assist and intersection movement assist, could prevent up to 592,000 crashes and save 1,083 lives per year.[7] Congestion could be significantly reduced by connected vehicle platooning, allowing more efficient capacity utilization. For instance, lane capacities could increase from 2,000 vehicles per hour to 8,000 vehicles per hour per travel lane.[8] USDOT estimated that a fully automated auto-mobile fleet can potentially increase highway capacity fivefold.[9] Morgan Stanley[10] predicts that autonomous vehicles could contribute $1.3 trillion in annual savings to the U.S. economy alone and $507 billion annually in productivity savings in the United States.

These advances are not decades away as some predict. There could be 10 million cars with semiautonomous and fully autonomous features on public roads by 2020, a tenfold increase from the current one million vehicles.[11]

## NATIONAL FOCUS ON ADOPTION OF PERFORMANCE MEASURES

In addition to advances in vehicle technology, the U.S. Department of Transportation, Federal Highway Administration (FHWA), and state departments of transportation have been progressively adopting transportation performance-management principles and measures to strategically use transportation system information to make investment and policy decisions to achieve performance goals. Since the passage of the Moving Ahead for Progress in the 21st Century Act (MAP-21) in July 2012, and the subsequent Fixing America's Surface Transportation Act (FAST) in December 2015, FHWA has worked collaboratively with stakeholders to adopt numerous performance metrics to support transportation missions and goals, measure performance, and show performance trends. In 2014 federal agencies began the rulemaking process for:

1. Safety performance measures
2. Highway safety improvement programs
3. Statewide and regional planning
4. Pavement and bridge performance measures
5. Transportation asset management plans.
6. System performance measures[12]

Although all of these programs can have significant impact on the future of transportation infrastructure and operations, two areas—safety and system performance—can significantly impact mobility into the future.

## SAFETY PERFORMANCE MEASURES

The Highway Safety Improvement Program (HSIP) is a federal transportation program with the purpose to reduce fatalities and serious injuries on all public roads by working with state and local transportation agencies. The HSIP requires a data-driven, strategic approach to improving highway safety on all public roads that focuses on performance. The HSIP requires DOTs to describe their progress toward achieving safety outcomes and performance targets and an overview of general highway safety trends. The Safety Performance Management Rule includes specific safety performance measure requirements to support the HSIP to assess and reduce serious injuries and fatalities on all public roads. The Safety PM Rule establishes five performance measures as the five-year rolling averages for:

1. Number of fatalities
2. Rate of fatalities per 100 million vehicle miles traveled (VMT)
3. Number of serious injuries
4. Rate of serious injuries per 100 million VMT
5. Number of nonmotorized fatalities and nonmotorized serious injuries[13]

It also establishes the process for agencies to report their safety targets, and to assess whether agencies have met or made significant progress toward meeting their safety targets.

The Safety PM Rule was implemented to improve safety data, foster transparency and accountability in safety measure reporting, and allow safety progress to be tracked at the national level. In support of the HSIP, the safety performance measures will inform planning, project programming, and decision making for the greatest possible reduction in fatalities and serious injuries and support of the USDOT toward zero deaths (TZD) vision.[14]

## SYSTEM PERFORMANCE MEASURES

The FHWA is currently proposing the use of two measures to evaluate National Highway System (NHS) performance—travel time reliability and peak hour travel time.[15] Each state DOT would calculate

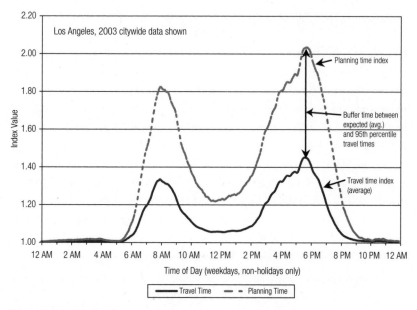

**Figure 8.2** Reliability Measures Compared to Average Congestion Measures
*Source: https://ops.fhwa.dot.gov/publications/tt_reliability/brochure/ttr_brochure.pdf.*

for reporting the level of travel time reliability (LOTTR) identified as the 80th percentile travel time divided by the 50th percentile (normal) travel time for each segment of NHS. Figure 8.2 illustrates the measures of the critical percentile travel times for a road segment.

If the calculated value for each segment is less than 1.5, that segment of NHS is considered to provide reliable travel times. DOTs will be required to report the percent of the interstate system with reliable travel times, and the percent of non-interstate NHS with reliable travel times.

Additionally, state DOTs must calculate the peak hour travel-time ratio (PHTTR) for each segment of the NHS within urbanized areas with populations over one million using the highest peak hour travel time from the annual average morning and afternoon periods, divided by the desired peak period travel time (established by the state DOT).[16] If the calculated value for each segment of urbanized NHS is less than 1.5, that segment of NHS is considered to provide reliable peak hour travel times. DOTs will be required to report the percent of the interstate providing reliable peak hour travel times, and the percent of non-interstate NHS with reliable peak hour travel times.[17]

## THE ROLE OF DATA AND ANALYTICS

The FHWA, in cooperation with state DOTs, has implemented a significant expansion of safety data collection to support analysis and decision making beyond the existing fatal accident reporting requirements. This expansion includes the types of public roadways where additional data is collected, types of data included in the collection, geolocation of safety data to a common roadway map, and the fundamental data elements to collect. States must be able to collect all crash data, roadway geometry data, traffic data, vehicle licensing data, and able to link or combine this data with other state core safety systems, as well as the national Fatality Analysis Reporting System (FARS). This expansion will enhance the ability of DOTs to identify safety problems and countermeasures, identify hazardous locations and severity, adopt performance goals while considering user impacts, and aid in the assessment of results achieved. Through this data-expansion effort, FHWA and state DOTs seek to achieve more informed decision making, that leads to improved targeted investment in safety projects and programs, and results in fewer fatalities and serious injuries. This enhanced data-driven safety analysis will increase a DOT's ability to predict specific roadway safety performance and quantify improvement impacts similar to the current methods of quantifying traffic growth or environmental impacts.[18]

This data enhancement will also assist in the systematic analysis of the roadway network to identify high-risk features correlated with severe crash types. This allows agencies to target system improvements over large areas, still targeting only those locations with the identified features.

In measuring travel time reliability and performance measures, the National Performance Management Research Data Set (NPMRDS) will be the data of record, which includes actual, observed passenger vehicle and truck travel times for all 230,000 miles of the National Highway System (NHS) measured every five minutes. These measures are recorded for all NHS segments, which can range from 0.1 miles in length in urban areas, to up to 10-mile-long segments in rural areas. The dataset currently contains less than a terabyte of historic travel time data for the NHS, with monthly updates averaging five to six gigabytes distributed to state DOTs. The NPMRDS was originally used to produce the FHWA Urban Congestion Trends Report that provided the state of congestion and reliability in the largest urban areas of the United States. Moving forward the NPMRDS will be the data set of record for measuring the travel-time performance of individual roadway segments, individual roadways, and the entire National Highway System. The Wisconsin Department of Transportation is actively using the NPMRDS to measure travel time and perform travel time analysis to produce the WisDOT Travel Time Reliability and Delay Report. Figures 8.3 and 8.4 are sample products from analyses of travel times using NPMRDS data on Wisconsin freeways.[19]

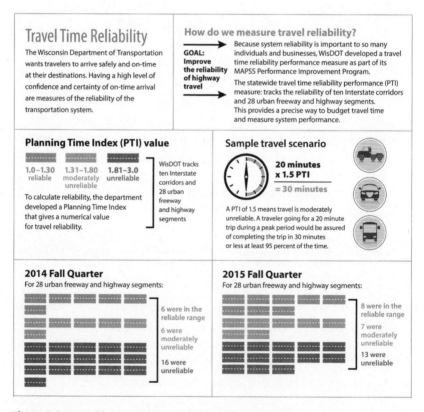

**Figure 8.3** Statewide Travel Time Reliability and Delay Report
*Source: Wisconsin Department of Transportation, http://wisconsindot.gov/Documents/about-wisdot/performance/mapss/travel-time-report-fall-2015.pdf.*

# Milwaukee Area Travel Time Reliability (Worst Peak)

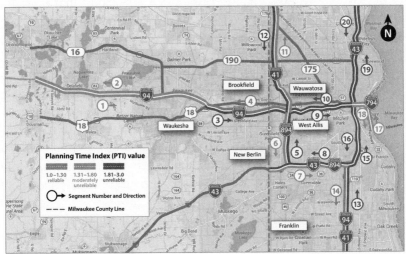

**Milwaukee Freeway Peak Travel Times:** 2015 Fall Quarter

| Map Link | Planning Time Index (PTI) | Highway | From | To | Distance Miles | Normal Travel Time Minutes | Worst Peak Travel Time Minutes | Worst Peak |
|---|---|---|---|---|---|---|---|---|
| 1 | 1.35 | I-94 EB | WIS 67 | US 18 | 15.5 | 13.3 | 17.9 | PM |
| 2 | 1.66 | I-94 WB | US 18 | WIS 67 | 15.5 | 13.3 | 22.1 | PM |
| 3 | 2.53 | I-94 EB | US 18 | Zoo interchange | 7.2 | 7.8 | 19.7 | PM |
| 4 | 1.29 | I-94 WB | Zoo interchange | US 18 | 7.0 | 7.0 | 9.1 | PM |
| 5 | 3.26 | I-894 WB | Hale interchange | Zoo interchange | 4.7 | 5.1 | 16.7 | AM |
| 6 | 1.75 | I-894 EB | Zoo interchange | Hale interchange | 4.5 | 4.9 | 8.6 | PM |
| 7 | 1.73 | I-43NB/894EB | Waukesha County Line | Mitchell interchange | 7.5 | 8.2 | 14.2 | AM |
| 8 | 1.85 | I-43SB/894WB | Mitchell interchange | Waukesha County Line | 7.0 | 7.6 | 14.1 | PM |
| 9 | 2.87 | I-94 EB | Zoo interchange | Marquette interchange | 5.6 | 6.4 | 18.4 | AM |
| 10 | 2.76 | I-94 WB | Marquette interchange | Zoo interchange | 5.8 | 6.6 | 18.2 | PM |
| 11 | 1.60 | US 45 NB | Zoo interchange | Waukesha County Line | 9.8 | 10.7 | 17.1 | PM |
| 12 | 3.17 | US 45 SB | Waukesha County Line | Zoo interchange | 9.8 | 10.7 | 33.9 | PM |
| 13 | 1.82 | I-94 WB | Racine County Line | Mitchell interchange | 8.6 | 8.1 | 14.7 | AM |
| 14 | 1.15 | I-94 EB | Mitchell interchange | Racine County Line | 8.8 | 8.2 | 9.5 | PM |
| 15 | 2.35 | I-94 WB | Mitchell interchange | Marquette interchange | 5.7 | 6.3 | 14.8 | AM |
| 16 | 2.19 | I-94 EB | Marquette interchange | Mitchell interchange | 5.9 | 6.5 | 14.2 | PM |
| 17 | 1.59 | I-794 WB | Carferry Dr | Marquette interchange | 3.6 | 4.3 | 6.9 | AM |
| 18 | 1.64 | I-794 EB | Marquette interchange | Carferry Dr | 3.5 | 4.2 | 6.9 | AM |
| 19 | 2.22 | I-43 NB | Marquette interchange | Ozaukee County Line | 11.0 | 12.1 | 26.8 | PM |
| 20 | 2.39 | I-43 SB | Ozaukee County Line | Marquette interchange | 10.9 | 12.2 | 29.2 | PM |

**Figure 8.4** Milwaukee Area Travel Time Reliability and Delay Report
*Source: Wisconsin Department of Transportation, http://wisconsindot.gov/Documents/about-wisdot/performance/mapss/travel-time-report-fall-2015.pdf.*

## BENEFITS OF TRANSPORTATION PERFORMANCE MANAGEMENT AND IMPROVED MEASURES

Performance measures and collected data allow agencies to use performance information to manage activities, communicate performance, and support the allocation of resources and decision making. The increased use of performance-based management with analytics and real-time data will improve performance and public accountability. Enhancements to safety performance measures will allow a significant expansion of safety analytics and data-driven decision making, nationally and at state and local levels. Visualization tools, such as the FHWA Roadway Safety Dashboard,[20] will allow expanded visualization and analysis of more complex data sets. Enhanced system-performance measures will allow for more efficient system improvements targeting specific recurring bottlenecks for the greatest network improvement, near real-time data analysis of streaming data for optimal signal timing and phasing throughout the road network, not just on individual priority corridors.

Nationally, federal transportation funds have historically been distributed on the basis of formula allocations, such as population or the number of bridges or lane-miles on the National Highway System. With future advances in the implementation of performance measures, future funding models might have a direct linkage to transportation-system performance, and substantially improve measured outcomes and resource utilization.

**PROFILE**

**Major General (Ret.) Jim Trogdon** is secretary of the N.C. Department of Transportation. Previously, he served as national transportation director for state and local government for SAS Institute. At SAS, he led the efforts to make America's roadways safer, more modern, and more cost effective through the use of analytics and business intelligence software. A professional engineer with 30 years of experience in transportation, 5 of them serving as chief operating officer at the North Carolina Department of Transportation, he was responsible for one of the nation's largest state transportation networks, with over 80,000 miles of highways and 17,000 bridges, and led an organization with a $4.4 billion annual budget and more than 13,000 employees. General Trogdon has a master's degree in Strategic Studies from the U.S. Army War College, as well as master's and bachelor's degrees in Civil Engineering from North Carolina State University.

# NOTES

1. U.S. Department of Transportation, *Transportation Statistics Annual Report 2015*, Bureau of Transportation Statistics (Washington, DC: 2016), www.rita.dot.gov/bts/sites/rita.dot.gov.bts/files/TSAR_2015_final_0.pdf.

2. Ibid.

3. U.S. Department of Transportation, "Beyond Traffic, Trends and Choices 2045," (September 2016), www.transportation.gov/sites/dot.gov/files/docs/Draft_Beyond_Traffic_Framework.pdf.

4. SAE International, "Automated Driving: Levels of Driving Automation Are Defined in New SAE International Standard J3016," www.sae.org/misc/pdfs/automated_driving.pdf.

5. Google Self-Driving Car Project, *Monthly Report* (July 2016), www.google.com/selfdrivingcar/reports/.

6. National Highway Traffic Safety Administration, "Federal Automated Vehicles Policy: Accelerating the Next Revolution in Roadway Safety," U.S. Department of Transportation (September 2016), www.transportation.gov/AV.

7. Federal Motor Vehicle Safety Standards: Vehicle-to-Vehicle (V2V) Communications; National Highway Traffic Safety Administration (NHTSA), Department of Transportation (DOT) Advance Notice of Proposed Rulemaking (ANPRM); Notice of Availability of Technical Report, 79 Fed. Reg. 161 (August 20, 2014).

8. Robert Campbell and Vassili Alexiadis, "Connected Vehicle Impacts on Transportation Planning: Analysis of the Need for New and Enhanced Analysis Tools, Techniques, and Data—Highway Capacity Manual Briefing," U.S. Department of Transportation (March 2, 2016), http://ntl.bts.gov/lib/59000/59300/59316/FHWA-JPO-16-365.pdf.

9. U.S. Department of Transportation, "Beyond Traffic, Trends and Choices 2045."

10. Morgan Stanley, "Autonomous Cars: The Futures Is Now," Morgan Stanley Blue Paper (January 23, 2015), www.morganstanley.com/articles/autonomous-cars-the-future-is-now/.

11. Motley Fool, "11 Facts About Driverless Cars Every Investor Should Know," *Nasdaq.com* (October 11, 2016), www.nasdaq.com/aspx/stockmarketnewsstoryprint.aspx?storyid=11-facts-about-driverless-cars-every-investor-should-know-cm692132.

12. U.S. Department of Transportation, Transportation Performance Management Rule Making Implementation Schedule, www.fhwa.dot.gov/TPM/.

13. "National Performance Management Measures: Highway Safety Improvement Program," *Federal Register* (March 15, 2016), www.federalregister.gov/documents/2016/03/15/2016-05202/national-performance-management-measures-highway-safety-improvement-program.

14. Ibid.

15. U.S. Department of Transportation, "National Performance Management Measures NPRM," Federal Highway Administration (April 2016), www.fhwa.dot.gov/tpm/rule/prespmoverview200416.pdf.

16. Ibid.

17. U.S. Department of Transportation, "Assessing Performance of the National Highway System, Freight Movement on the Interstate System, and the Congestion Mitigation and Air Quality Improvement Program," Federal Highway Administration (April 2016). www.fhwa.dot.gov/tpm/rule/systemperf20042016.pdf.

18. U.S. Department of Transportation, "Data-Driven Safety Analysis Resources," Federal Highway Administration, www.fhwa.dot.gov/innovation/everydaycounts/edc-3/ddsa_resources/.

19. Wisconsin Department of Transportation, "Travel Time Reliability and Delay Report," (Fall 2015), wisconsindot.gov/Documents/about-wisdot/performance/mapss/travel-time-report-fall-2015.pdf.

20. U.S. Department of Transportation, "Roadway Safety Data Dashboards," Federal Highway Administration, rspcb.safety.fhwa.dot.gov/Dashboard/Default.aspx.

CHAPTER **9**

# Fraud, Waste, and Abuse

*Carl Hammersburg*

Overworked, understaffed, and under attack. In many ways, that is what an average day in government feels like for staff who are tasked with ensuring that taxes are reported and paid by individuals and businesses and tax dollars don't go out the door to the wrong people. Worse yet, the lens of citizens applies a Goldilocks filter, as I have come to refer to it. Pay anything inappropriately, and you are being too easy; audit or investigate the wrong person or company, and you're being too hard and imposing a government burden.

The rise of computers and the Internet has brought many improvements. I remember when I submitted my tax returns to the IRS on paper, and waited months for a check back in the mail. Now, I submit things online quickly, and have a refund deposited directly to my bank account within weeks.

At the same time, these advances have opened up all of these programs to many more threats in terms of fraud. Identity theft for purposes of committing government fraud has risen dramatically in recent years. When the Federal Trade Commission issued its annual report on consumer complaints in February 2015, the top complaint was identity theft, and using stolen identities for government fraud (39 percent) exceeded credit card (17 percent) and bank account fraud (8 percent) together.[1] Programs suddenly saw funding for standard audits and investigations diverted to tackle cybersecurity and identity theft issues. While the right response, overall it represented another hit to the ability to protect program funding and tax collection.

Putting the risks into hard numbers, here are a few statistics:

- The Internal Revenue Service (IRS) reports a tax gap every five years. This is their best estimate of taxes that are under-reported or underpaid. Their report released in 2016 put that gap at $458 billion annually,[2] and that's looking back at the average from tax years 2008–2010, meaning the problem has only grown since then.

- Respected economists Edgar Feige and Richard Cebula, in looking at the underground economy, estimated a few years ago that more than $2 trillion[3,4] in economic activity is unreported in the United States annually.

- In Washington State, taxing agencies teamed up to study the impact of the underground economy, which was calculated at nearly $708 million in unpaid business taxes annually.[5]

- Medicaid improper payment rates came in at 9.8 percent for 2015, or $29.1 billion,[6] and that's just based on audits and known errors. Worse yet, the target for 2016 is a rise to an 11.5 percent improper payment rate.

## HEALTHCARE

More than any other programs, government healthcare programs like Medicaid and Medicare in the United States, and their counterparts internationally, are under constant attack from fraudsters. Cases run into the millions so regularly that it is impossible to go a single day without another new conviction or charges filed for a multimillion-dollar fraud scheme.

The latest of the largest fraud cases in history racked up $900 million in fraud from one network, with 301 individuals arrested in June 2016[7] as part of actions by the Medicare Fraud Task Force. While it is critical that the task force was successful in bringing these individuals to justice and plugging a gaping hole, what can be taken away from this bust? A few thoughts:

### Positives
- Multiple federal and state agencies coordinated enforcement efforts.
- Data sharing was occurring between multiple entities at both the state and federal level.

### Negatives
- While some claims were prevented, hundreds of millions of dollars were paid out fraudulently before detection and prevention took place.

The collaboration that took place in this case does represent government at its best. Too often, programs refuse to share data, claiming legal barriers. In my own experience, those decisions are often made by individuals who are tasked solely with protecting data, without solid legal analysis or including the individuals responsible for protecting government programs at risk.

During my time working for Washington State, one of the most important things I learned was to read and reread the laws on the books, and consider how they can be followed but also utilized to succeed. In some cases, that analysis led to work with our Attorney General's Office and other agencies that enabled new data sharing to prevent fraud and improve compliance. In other cases, it helped us truly understand the barriers and take those forward to stakeholders and elected officials for discussion. That open discussion enabled changes to definitions and data-sharing laws to help bring consistency and improve the fight against fraud.

More could have been done with data to help detect and prevent this fraud and reduce the total costs to the citizens and taxpayers of the United States. The federal government understands this as well, and made two important changes in recent years. The first allows state Medicaid fraud control units (MFCUs) to use data mining and analytics to proactively detect fraud and take action. The second allows the use of tax records from the IRS to help prevent fraud in any benefits programs that include federal funds. That includes not only state-run, but largely federally funded programs like Medicaid, but also unemployment programs, food assistance (Supplemental Nutrition Assistance Program or SNAP), and cash assistance (Temporary Assistance for Needy Families or TANF).

These are both truly critical changes to federal restrictions that open up many avenues for improvement. So, there must be many success stories to tell as a result, correct? Not quite. I have yet to encounter a single benefits program at the state level that has actually started utilizing the IRS for fraud and identity theft detection.

While some MFCUs have started down the route of acquiring and utilizing data mining and analytics software for purposes of proactive fraud detection, this work remains in its infancy and most states have taken no steps to make this happen. Failing to be proactive at both the agency level within health and human services programs, as well as oversight and protection units like MFCUs, are what allow cases to grow into the millions in terms of losses.

Some states are taking steps to stem the tide, improving their use of data and analytics. Many are currently in a cycle of replacement of their core claims processing systems, and associated functions that handle data. A trend of modularizing those and giving a strong focus to improving the use of data and embedding analytics for improving health outcomes and reducing costs as well as preventing fraud and improper payments started in the last couple of years and continues to increase. Colorado, Kansas, Missouri, and South Carolina are just a few examples of states that have already started such projects, or will be starting them soon.

Other states have taken the wakeup call of auditors' reports as a call for change, and moved specifically on fraud analytics. One of those is Massachusetts, which seized on uproar concerning improper payments and used that as a catalyst for acquiring new analytics capabilities. A new system, implemented three years ago, showed over $2 million in savings in the first six months[8] alone. Over time, these types of results enable the systems to pay for themselves, and begin helping the positive ROI of the entire program.

Health programs are rich with data, and analytics can and should be applied at various points:

- Eligibility determination for recipients
- Enrollment of providers
- Ongoing reverification of eligibility for recipients
- Prepayment on claims by providers
- Post-payment/longer-term analytics

By implementing an analytical program in a phased manner that addresses all of these points, significant savings can be achieved before costs and payments mount. It also allows for analysis that requires patterns to develop over time. Verifying rules, treatments that can't occur in conjunction (for example, in home care the same day as inpatient hospital treatments), outlier analysis on volumes, treatment patterns, and diagnoses provide a range of tools to stop fraud and abuse. Layer on the analysis of referral networks, prescription behaviors, and other connections, and the $900 million case likely would have been stopped at a much lower cost.

## TAX AND THE UNDERGROUND ECONOMY

These days, tax programs face serious challenges from multiple angles. The traditional schemes of underreporting income, participating in the underground economy as referenced by Edward Feige, and false deductions are exploding. Information released from the Panama Papers scandal[9] covered one method of this type of tax evasion, aided by hiding assets offshore. The documents revealed schemes by current and former heads of state, their families, and many noted celebrities, and led to the prime minister of Iceland[10] resigning as part of the fallout from the scandal and release of information. Taxing agencies around the world were already well aware of these gaps, and voluntary disclosure programs for offshore assets netted $8 billion to the IRS between 2009 and late 2015.[11]

There is an ongoing erosion of underlying honesty and belief that taxes should be paid, as well as acceptance of other forms of fraud that involve concepts like "sticking it to the man," otherwise describing entities like governments and insurance companies. A couple of surveys are emblematic of this. In one, conducted by the Insurance Research Council, 24 percent[12] of people surveyed in the United States believe it is acceptable to commit insurance fraud. In a second survey, conducted globally, about 1 in 5 workers said they would sell their passwords[13] to their employer's systems, 44 percent of them for amounts less than $1,000, and many as low as $100. The United States fared even worse in that survey, with more than 1 in 4 willing to do the same. These aren't positive trends for voluntary reporting of income and payment of taxes.

At the same time, the explosion of hacking and the global persistence of the Internet and systems connected to it has caused a massive increase in identity theft worldwide. While data is spotty in other countries, and the FTC report mentioned earlier captures just a small subset of all identity theft victims, research shows 13.1 million identity-theft victims in the United States in 2015,[14] or 1 every 2 seconds. Think about that. While you are reading this single paragraph, multiple people in the United States had their identities stolen. With 39 percent of those being utilized for fraudulent purposes within government programs, many of those attacks now go toward the IRS or state revenue agencies in the form of false refund requests.

As with other programs, one of the first lines of defense is using data wisely and data sharing. The good news here is that taxing agencies are much further ahead than their counterparts in this respect. While not every U.S. state has state-level income tax—my home state of Washington is one of the exceptions—all 50 U.S. states and the District of Columbia are allowed to share and receive tax data from the IRS on both individuals and business. That sharing provides an excellent check and balance on fraud at the state and federal levels, both in terms of traditional tax evasion as well as fraud from identity theft. Discrepancies between data quickly point to fake claims and statements.

Many states are taking it a step further, and bounce data against their state unemployment or workforce agencies. That sharing helps to reduce fraud and tax evasion within both the general revenue programs and unemployment tax reporting, and assists with uncovering individual fraud and underground economy activity from businesses.

There are some examples where data sharing has gone even further. One of those includes work I did in Washington State. There, data from the government workers' compensation program was matched with sales and business revenue taxes, unemployment, data from the department of licensing, corporate filings with the secretary of state, and many other programs. While not every program could receive all data in return, leads could still be provided to many other compliance programs, multiplying the value of data, analytics, and audits performed in other programs. This approach helped take audits with positive outcomes from a rate of around 50 percent in the mid-2000s to 81 to 85 percent in recent years. That's a win that brings much higher outcomes from the same number of staff, while reducing the burden of an audit on compliant employers. Ultimately, that's what the goal of government compliance programs should be—minimizing the burden on businesses and taxpayers by spending time on those who aren't following the law.

Another example is the Government Data Analytics Center (GDAC) in North Carolina. That center pulls together multiple data sets from state programs in order to tackle hard problems. It grew out of work that initially pulled together criminal justice data to assist courts and law enforcement officers, then expanded to take on fraud and other government challenges. One public example of the results of this approach came in the form of a press release and article in

*GCN*[15] covering its use in workers' compensation coverage compliance. At the time, the head of the program touted this system as a huge shift from only discovering noncompliance when an employee was injured, leading to over 600 additional firms with coverage and more than $1 million in fines collected to date.

The IRS has long utilized analytics within its programs to identify fraud and identity theft. A system currently undergoing replacement was originally established in 2009. Recent results show significant impact, with nearly 2 million returns totaling over $14.9 billion[16] stopped in 2014 as a result of matching and analytics in place.

Analytics as well as data matching are critical, particularly in the cases of identity theft. Those cases require intervention prior to refund issuance, as the money is virtually impossible to claw back once it has gone out the door. That shifts all traditional methods on their head and turns tax agencies into entities that need to do prepayment detection and intervention, as opposed to auditing after the fact as with traditional tax evasion. This makes their work very similar to those of benefits agencies.

Proper analytics helps sift large piles of taxpayer returns to identify those who have elements of identity theft and do early intervention with a low level of staff time invested. At the same time, those systems can help identify top candidates for traditional compliance audits and intervention, or help move toward guided self-audits for low-level issues; this is a wise approach that balances limited resources and staff with a growing workload and challenge.

One of the greatest assets that taxing agencies do have going for them is their focus. As they normally exist solely to bring in revenue for government and ensure compliance, almost all have developed some form of rules-based fraud engine as well as the skills to go after compliance. Pivoting those assets to broader data sharing and analytics can happen much more quickly than in programs where compliance is a small component that isn't considered a core function.

## BENEFITS PROGRAMS

Benefits programs cover a wide range of different activities, from the more traditional ones like SNAP (food stamps) or TANF (welfare), to the less well-known programs like unemployment benefits, housing and heating subsidies, and subsidized child care. These are some of the most traditional government programs criticized for being rife with fraud, without real data or proof in the hands of average citizens. Actual audits show much lower rates of improper payments in many of these programs than in others, like unemployment, Medicaid, and Medicare, but still show the opportunity for hundreds of millions or billions in potential savings nationally.

Barriers exist in many of these programs to really make progress on the prevention of fraud and improper payments. In the United States' SNAP program, for example, much of the fraud involves collusion and selling of benefits cards from recipients to fraudulent grocery stores/vendors. However, responsibility for auditing or investigating vendors lies with the federal government, while the recipients are the responsibility of the states. Furthermore, the benefits are 100 percent federal, as opposed to a shared cost, reducing incentive for any state to spend their funds to improve detection or take action. As a result, innovation within this program is lagging.

Unemployment is a program ripe for action, as costs are shared between the federal government and the states, and there are regular grants issued by the United States Department of Labor for improving systems and staffing to prevent improper payments and fraud. Plus, with an improper payment rate standing at 10.7 percent and $3.5 billion in 2015,[17] there is much room for improvement.

Numerous states have taken steps to stem the tide. Increasingly, they have adopted rules-based systems to assist in analysis and detection, and increase contacts with employers to verify wages when they suspect individuals are working at the same time they are collecting unemployment benefits. More are turning to third-party data providers to enrich what they know about claimants. Others are implementing tests based on third-party data to verify identity when a claim is filed as a method to cut down on identity theft.

States like Tennessee and others are matching with incarceration data, state employee payroll records, new hire databases, and vital records data as a way to discover situations in which someone wouldn't be eligible to receive benefits. Using advanced analytics to ensure that fuzzy identity matching happens as part of that process helps prevent false negatives from slight differences in how names are recorded or spelled, or typos, or intentional, small errors in Social Security numbers.

The state of North Carolina utilized analytics as the means to uncover a complex scheme of fake businesses that were formed expressly to file fraudulent unemployment claims. As reported by television station WRAL in Raleigh, the North Carolina Division of Employment Security took down 105 fake employers statewide, representing 672 fake claims filed,[18] and saved more than $5.2 million from being paid out. Again, this shows the value of tackling fraud strongly, being up front about the results, and using data to discover the problem.

While most of the large benefits programs are run or funded by states, some with support and funding from the federal government, there are times when counties are involved as well. In larger population areas, cities and counties sometimes operate significant programs of their own. One example of a county that saw a fraud problem and chose to tackle it is Los Angeles County.

In particular, upon recognizing growing fraud and networks of fraud collusion, Los Angeles County chose to develop an analytics system that aggregated data from multiple systems and helped identify risks. The end result of that work was a 2015 GCN Award for IT Excellence, cutting the time to prosecute cases by 18 months and millions in annual cost savings.[19]

## RECOMMENDATIONS

While some recommendations apply more to specific programs, these are some of the key steps I would recommend to any government organization wishing to improve their rates of improper payments or reduce fraud, waste, and abuse:

- **Set a baseline**—You need to know how well you are doing today in order to measure improvement tomorrow and the day after. Measure not just one metric but many. We looked at the number of audits and investigations completed, outcomes like dollars identified, criminal charges and convictions, and many more. Measuring the percentage of time you audited or investigated the right person or case is critical. Best of all, calculate an ROI for the entire program. We measured the value of every dollar we collected or prevented at Washington Labor and Industries, divided by all the costs of the program, including administrative overhead. Knowing that value ranged from $8 up to $11 for every $1 spent helped show the value of the program.

- **Be public with your story**—One lesson I've learned is that if you aren't telling your story, someone else will make up their version and tell it for you. Once you know your numbers, and have plans in place, put that out to your executive management, stakeholders, and elected officials. When we took a mandatory annual report to the legislature that no one ever read and made it a visual story with all the details and plans laid out, put it online, and starting handing it out, it became a powerful tool. Fear of criticism of fraud leads too many organizations to choose not to discuss it, measure it, or talk about it. That only leads to stagnation and lack of success. Eventually the lack of action will be found by the public, oversight agencies, and auditors. The first time I saw a stakeholder raise our annual fraud report in his hand when testifying to the legislature and use that to show how hard we were working and that we needed more support, I knew we had changed the entire underlying story.

- **Learn the laws**—Find out all the tools you truly have at your disposal and what the barriers are. When I did that, I found some enforcement tools that had been on the books for decades that weren't being used. We started using them immediately. I also found and pushed the limits of what data could be shared with us, with other agencies, and with the public. By doing so, it enabled our agency to create an online system that allows anyone to verify if a business in Washington is registered for workers' compensation,[20] their approximate size, and the type of work they do. This became a force multiplier, as competitors turned in illegal businesses, union representatives turned in bad construction contractors, and the general public turned away from many unregistered businesses.

- **Share, share, share**—There's an important reason why so many examples mention this. It's truly one of the best steps government agencies can take to protect themselves and one another. Look at the laws, find out the limits, and see what can be done. There are many ways to follow privacy restrictions. Some of my staff could utilize IRS data, while others couldn't. The IRS and other state agencies had the authority to audit us and our use of their data. Strict access and log controls were in place. In other situations, there may be a way to gain insights without sharing the details. For example, knowing just the relative size of a business according to data from another agency, whether in terms of sales, employment, or other measure may be enough to know if you should audit that business or not. That is an amazing insight without sharing one detail of the underlying data reported. At an even higher level, it could be one-way sharing when that is the only way possible and just a question to that other program: "Do you think we have a problem?" Be thoughtful about different approaches to the challenge of sharing.

- **Analyze data**—While matching is great, true insights come from applying analytics and moving beyond simple black and white rules. This can be true even if you have no data from outside your own program. Many examples exist that show this approach can bring great value, yet most state agencies are in their infancy.

After heading down the paths I recommend, you can take on the other challenges, like staffing limitations, true legal limits on enforcement tools, or data sharing. By coming with all the information in hand, and showing what you can accomplish within current constraints and the ROI that produces, the conversation with elected officials is far different.

Not one program that has seen success hasn't faced the same problems I see in government programs everywhere. Staffing is almost always constrained or significantly short for the task at hand and the vast majority had at least some antiquated computer systems underlying them. That just shows what is possible for everyone.

**PROFILE**

▼ **Carl Hammersburg** is manager in Government and Healthcare Risk and Fraud, Security Intelligence, at SAS Institute. For 26 years, he has been working in government healthcare, tax audit, and collections, and antifraud efforts. Prior to joining SAS, he worked for Washington State, where he evangelized data-sharing and partnering between government tax and regulatory efforts within the state and with federal partners. Hammersburg also oversaw the Fraud Prevention and Compliance Program for Washington Labor and Industries, driving an ROI of $9:$1 while doubling audits and investigations and tripling outcomes, earning awards from two successive governors. He received his B.S. from the University of Washington.

## NOTES

1. Federal Trade Commission, *Consumer Sentinel Network Data Book for January–December 2014* (February 2015), www.ftc.gov/system/files/documents/reports/consumer-sentinel-network-data-book-january-december-2014/sentinel-cy2014-1.pdf.

2. Internal Revenue Service, Tax Gap Estimates for Tax Years 2008–2010 (April 2016), www.irs.gov/PUP/newsroom/tax%20gap%20estimates%20for%202008%20through%202010.pdf.

3. Richard Cebula and Edgar L. Feige, "America's Underground Economy: Measuring the Size, Growth and Determinants of Income Tax Evasion in the U.S." (2013), http://www.lhc.ca.gov/studies/226/March%20Testimony/Hammersburg%20Attachments/Attachment%20A.pdf.

4. Brad Plumer, "The $2 Trillion Shadow Economy in the Recession's Big Winner," *Washington Post* (April 23, 2013), www.washingtonpost.com/news/wonk/wp/2013/04/23/americas-2-trillion-shadow-economy-is-the-recessions-big-winner/.

5. Lorrie Brown, Stan Harris, James Callen, and Lael Byington, "Unregistered Business Study,"Joint Report of the Washington State Department of Revenue, Washington State Department of Labor and Industries, and the Washington State Employment Security Department (November 2007), www.lni.wa.gov/Main/Docs/JointUnregBusinessStudyNov2007.pdf.

6. Payment Accuracy. (2015). Medicaid. Retrieved from https://paymentaccuracy.gov/program/medicaid/.

7. U.S. Department of Justice, "National Health Care Fraud Takedown Results in Charges Against 301 Individuals for Approximately $900 Million in False Billing," Office of Public Affairs (June 22, 2016), www.justice.gov/opa/pr/national-health-care-fraud-takedown-results-charges-against-301-individuals-approximately-900.

8. Rutrell Yasin, "How MassHealth Cut Medicaid Fraud With Predictive Analytics," GCN.com (February 24, 2014), gcn.com/articles/2014/02/24/masshealth.aspx.

9. The International Consortium of Investigative Journalists, "Giant Leak of Offshore Financial Records Exposes Global Array of Crime and Corruption," Organized Crime and Corruption Reporting Project (April 3, 2016), www.occrp.org/en/panamapapers/overview/intro/.

10. Steven Erlanger, Stephen Castle, and Rick Gladstone, "Iceland's Prime Minister Steps Down Amid Panama Papers Scandal," *New York Times*, April 5, 2016, www .nytimes.com/2016/04/06/world/europe/panama-papers-iceland.html?_r=1.

11. U.S. Internal Revenue Service, "Offshore Compliance Programs Generate $8 Billion; IRS Urges People to Take Advantage of Voluntary Disclosure Programs," IRS.gov (October 16, 2015), www.irs.gov/uac/newsroom/offshore-compliance-programs -generate-8-billion-irs-urges-people-to-take-advantage-of-voluntary-disclosure -programs.

12. David Corum, "New Study Finds Lower Acceptance of Insurance Fraud and Strong Support for Fraud-Fighting Efforts," Insurance Research Council (March 23, 2013), www.insurance-research.org/sites/default/files/downloads/ PressReleaseDraftMarch12.pdf.

13. Jonathan Chew, "One in Five Employees Would Sell Their Work Passwords," Fortune.com (March 30, 2016), http://fortune.com/2016/03/30/passwords-sell -poor-sailpoint/.

14. Al Pascual, Kyle Marchini, and Sarah Miller, "2016 Identity Fraud: Fraud Hits an In- flection Point," Javelin Strategy.com (February 2, 2016), https://www.javelinstrategy .com/coverage-area/2016-identity-fraud-fraud-hits-inflection-point.

15. Amanda Ziadeh, "Data Sharing Helps North Carolina Detect Workers' Comp Fraud," GCN.com (August 6, 2015), gcn.com/articles/2015/08/06/workers-comp-fraud -detection.aspx.

16. Meta S. Brown, "Analytics and the IRS: A New Way to Find Cheaters," Forbes.com (January 28, 2016), www.forbes.com/sites/metabrown/2016/01/28/analytics-and -the-irs-a-new-way-to-find-cheaters/#4d9c69ac5b8b.

17. Department of Labor, "Payment Accuracy," Unemployment Insurance (2015), https://paymentaccuracy.gov/program/unemployment-insurance/.

18. Cullen Browder, "Fake Companies, Fake Workers: State Battling New Type of Unemployment Fraud." WRAL.com (February 3, 2015), www.wral.com/fake -companies-fake-workers-state-battling-new-type-of-unemployment-fraud/ 14414281/.

19. Paul McCloskey, "LA County Unravels a Web of Child Care Fraud," GCN.com (October 19, 2015), https://gcn.com/articles/2015/10/19/gcna-la-child-care-fraud .aspx?s=gcntech_201015.

20. Washington State Department of Labor and Industries, "Verify a Contractor, Trades- person or Business," https://secure.lni.wa.gov/verify/.

# CHAPTER 10

# Center of Analytics

*Kay Meyer*

doctoral engineering student from India, nearly ready to take his PhD-qualifying exams, is murdered in his apartment near the campus of a prominent American university. Just weeks later, the student body president and recipient of a prestigious scholarship at a neighboring university is kidnapped and murdered. Similar to 9/11, the investigation into these murders revealed that law enforcement, probation, and the courts had key information about the suspects—information with the potential to have changed the ultimate outcome for these two students—but that data was isolated across multiple criminal justice systems, making it difficult and time consuming to access and review.

This tragic series of events demonstrates the need to change our way of thinking and our way of using data. My team and I were tasked with fixing this problem in our criminal justice community by building an integrated, statewide criminal justice system—a single system to provide comprehensive profiles of offenders and enable alerting on changes in offender status. The objective was to put critical information into the hands of law enforcement, courts, and correction personnel and enhance their efforts to manage, locate, and interact with the offender population and, most importantly, improve public safety.

While the reason for developing the system was based on tragedy, the development and implementation of the system was one of the most fulfilling experiences of my career. Through close and constant engagement with key stakeholders in the criminal justice system, and partnership with the technology vendor, we built a robust, accurate, and easy-to-use system with the power to transform the work of criminal justice professionals in the state.

▶ **EXTRACT**

Once we know something, we find it hard to imagine what it was like not to know it.

Chip and Dan Heath, authors of *Made to Stick*, introduction
(New York: Random House, 2007); and *Switch* (New York: Random House, 2010).

---

This initial criminal justice effort laid the foundation for my state's enterprise analytics center of excellence—that resulted in enterprise fraud, waste, and compliance solutions, healthcare analysis, financial and procurement reporting, and so much more. An enterprise vision and approach has the power to revolutionize government's insight and understanding—knowing the who, the why, the how often and how much, the what if, and so much more, to change the way we operate, interact with our citizens, and impact the world around us.

As you've read the chapters of this book, you've seen examples of *when government knows better it can do better*—how data, and the ability to gain insights into that data through data integration and the use of analytics, can transform government services and operations. With the great potential in data that we've collected over the years as well as infinite possibilities in new types of data available now, we are just beginning to scratch the surface of what this data can do for us. In fact, the Gartner 2017 CIO Agenda, based on a survey of public and private sector CIOs worldwide, listed business intelligence and analytics as the top priority investment for CIOs for the sixth year in a row.[1]

I believe that we all strive to be more effective and efficient in our work—to be better leaders, better teachers, better doctors, better social workers, better at whatever we do. Unfortunately with many challenges in government, we are stifled by trying to solve the problem in isolation with limited data—information that provides only a part of the picture. Critical opportunities to improve government require better access to a broader range of data about businesses, people, and programs. Imagine a social worker trying to serve the needs of an at-risk child without insight into the child's whole environment, a fraud investigator who can only see the activity of a business within a single government sector, or a financial analyst who cannot see the impact of economic conditions on future revenues and budgets—their ability to make the best decisions will be limited. Comprehensive data and the ability to analyze and understand that data can enhance human judgment and experience and drive decisions based on information. So how do we help our government organizations evolve into data-driven organizations to meet the challenges highlighted in this book, transform the way we make decisions, improve our operations, and better serve our citizens?

▶ **EXTRACT**

In the 2016 NASCIO State CIO Survey, "58 percent of CIOs placed data governance and management as a high priority or essential element in achieving their goals and objectives."

"The 2016 State CIO Survey: The Adaptable State CIO," NASCIO, Grant Thornton, and CompTIA, September 2016.

From my many years in government information technology work, I have learned that acquiring and implementing technology for technology's sake or establishing a program without a clear vision of how the program will support key business needs rarely achieves the expected outcome. As demonstrated throughout this book, building an analytics-driven government must first focus on recognizing the compelling issues we face in serving our citizens—whether improving education, enhancing public safety, reducing fraud and wasteful spending, or making the way citizens interact with our government services more efficient. Then to ensure that we can effectively transform our business to meet these needs, we must establish an approach that facilitates data sharing, analytics, and business and technology process transformation across the business functions of government.

Throughout the nation, government is setting a strategy to leverage data assets in more effective ways and build stronger analytics capabilities. While some organizations continue to insist that we can't share data, many governments are exploring what it takes to make data sharing the norm. Organizations like the City of Boston's Citywide Analytics Team[2] and New York City's Mayor's Office of Data Analytics[3] seek innovative ways to leverage data in order to meet critical government business needs. Governors' Executive Orders and legislative language is helping to drive states toward data sharing and analytics programs. With the program in my own state, legislation drove the vision from early data sharing to develop an enterprise criminal justice system to ultimately establish the North Carolina Government Data Analytics Center. These targeted efforts promote, support, and build partnership between business units and technology teams, support improved data management, build engagement and use of analytics, and help government decrease expense and reduce redundancy in answering their most pressing social and economic issues.

So what is your next big business question? A center of analytics for government can help you answer that question, and many more, by breaking down the barriers to sharing and accessing information and developing and supporting solutions to ensure front-line workers, management, and policymakers have the knowledge they need to move from thought to action on key government issues.

## WHY A CENTER OF ANALYTICS?

A center of excellence is a program or organization that brings leadership, expertise, best practices, and implementation to meet particular objectives. We see centers of excellence used throughout industry to improve the operations and efficiencies in all areas of business. In healthcare, cancer centers of excellence are researching cures, advancing treatment and care, and improving outcomes in the lives of cancer patients. Customer centers of excellence provide responsive customer services, build brand loyalty, and seek to increase revenue through better alignment of marketing campaigns to customer interest. Supply chain centers of excellence focus on reduction in cost of inventory, improved distribution routes, and efficiency in the use of key plant and equipment resources. Whatever the business area, a center of excellence is focused on optimizing effort, reducing cost, and generating value through improved results. There is a great opportunity in government to leverage a center of analytics to increase the value of analytics projects and ensure greater opportunity for success.

A center of analytics (COA) provides a clearly defined program, staff, and resources to help government gain broader access to data, strategically manage analytics across the enterprise, and evolve to a mindset focused on the use of data and analysis to answer government's most difficult questions. While typical government IT projects are built in a siloed approach, with organizations using different technology, development, and project management approaches to develop IT solutions, a COA focuses on building common competency, successful and repeatable processes, governance, and efficiency. It enhances government analytic success through shared experience and learning, analytic synergy, and economies of scale across government agencies.

## WHAT MAKES A CENTER OF ANALYTICS?

While there are many variations on how a center of analytics can be defined and managed, a successful program will include several key components: mindset, people, process, and technology (Figure 10.1).

### Mindset

It begins with a vision and a strategy that is championed and evangelized by leadership of the organization—and *where leadership meets vision, the results can be remarkable*. Whether at the enterprise level, encompassing all government organizations, or more narrowly scoped, like an agency or division, the vision to move toward data-driven program management, resources, and activities must be clearly articulated and shared with the organization's personnel—from management to the front line workers. Leadership is critical in shaking up the status quo, voicing the message that while analytics will change the way we do business, the changes improve operations, enable better use of resources, and eliminate manual administrative work—not endangering jobs but allowing people to more effectively do the jobs they were trained to do.

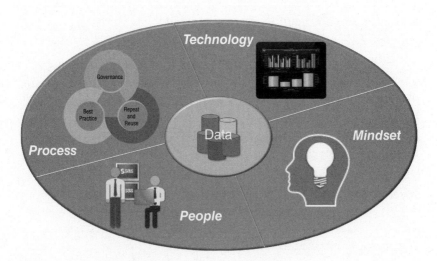

**Figure 10.1** Mindset, People, Process, and Technology

Transformation can be challenging so leadership's message must be reinforced with training, education, and support that engages and enables personnel throughout the organization to learn to use new analytic tools and solutions, to question and seek new insights in their day-to-day work, and to spend more time using their skills and knowledge rather than performing manual collection and assessment of information.

## People

I've found that rarely is technology the greatest challenge to enabling government transformation. More often the greatest inhibitor to using technology to change our business is a people factor. A COA can help address the people factor with a team approach—the right people, in the right roles, with the right motivation to help design, develop, and implement analytics solutions that drive businesses to change. Executive leadership has the influence and authority to actively recognize and support the mission to make data-driven decisions part of every aspect of government business. This leader identifies the political and business challenges and sets a strategy for resolving them. Strong leadership gives the program clear guidance and impetus for achieving measureable results. In building our criminal justice systems, our executive leader spent considerable time meeting with legislators, leadership in participating agencies, and our vendor partner to ensure we were all on the same page with commitment, expected outcomes, and timeline.

Stakeholders have a vested interest in solving a business problem or in sharing data to support problem solving. Stakeholders may own the business problem, act as steward of data resources needed to understand the problem, serve as legal or compliance experts in finding ways to share and govern data, or be the citizen population impacted by the analytic solution. Engaging key stakeholders early and consistently throughout the lifecycle of an analytics project is critical—from clear definition of the business problem to the final roll-out of a solution. These stakeholders play a key role in ensuring adoption and value of the solution. Criminal justice personnel from law enforcement, courts, and corrections—leaders as well as front-line workers—played a critical role in understanding how the data should be integrated into the system, determining the look and feel of screens to ensure information was easy to find, and to clearly define how the system would function in the field.

Strong technical resources, including business analysts, data scientists, and system administration personnel, bring the skills of business process analysis, data integration and statistical analysis, reporting and visualization, and system optimization. Perhaps most importantly, trainers and support personnel help teach end users how to leverage their new insights and take action accordingly.

## Process

Policies, procedures, and activities allow a COA to support the sharing of data and successfully implement analytic solutions.

Governance policy and procedure plays a key role when managing data assets across the enterprise. It improves the quality, consistency, and reliability of data and provides the control framework to enable data sharing and access. Data provided by different sources will vary in content, quality, and definition—a field called customer might mean the same thing as a field called client in another data source, mandatory fields might only contain valid values 60 percent of the time, and dates can come in a variety of formats. Governance establishes enterprise data standards that ensure that data content is clearly defined, consistent, and reliable.

Governance is also needed to ensure data privacy and security. When considering the concept of cross-agency analytics, data sharing is often the first objection—these objectives may be based on regulations or law, opinion that has become ingrained as fact, or simply the idea that it has never been done. At times, sensitive and highly confidential data, regulated by federal and state policy such as HIPAA,[4] Publication 1075,[5] FERPA,[6] and CJIS Security Policy,[7] may be needed to solve some of government's most complex business issues. An effective COA establishes strong governance policy to clearly define the purposes for which data can be used, enforces data access controls through user authentication and role-based security, and defines requirements for auditing data usage within the enterprise program. We established comprehensive, standardized policy based on understanding and compliance with state and federal regulations. Standard data access and usage agreements enabled broader access across departmental data and ensured that new analytic needs were not needlessly impacted by negotiations around data access. We created licensing and auditing procedures to ensure we closely managed who accessed data, controlled how that data was used, and had the ability to report the data usage to ensure compliance with our governance policy.

Best practices play a different role in a COA's success. We learn from our successes and our mistakes and often failure is an opportunity to learn. Best practices can be established from researching other people's efforts, but often building them from experience is the best possible way to ensure future success. Best practices can guide all aspects of analytic development from engaging project stakeholders, scoping and prioritizing projects, identifying required data sources, leveraging project-management methodologies, ensuring strong and consistent communications, and proactively planning for implementation and support. Best practice doesn't mean we can always avoid making a misstep, but it can mean not repeating one.

Repeat and reuse helps us avoid potential pitfalls and wasted time reinventing the wheel. Imagine expanding your home. When adding a new bathroom, you don't dig a new well and run new power lines to the electric grid—instead you add pipes and wiring to the existing infrastructure in your home. An enterprise COA can provide opportunity to build a component or capability or integrate a data source once, and then reuse it for new analytic needs. These reusable components and data save time, reduce maintenance, and ensure consistency across the enterprise. For example, after evaluating and developing user authentication and role-based security capabilities that integrated with our state's identity management systems, new solutions can incorporate these capabilities in a fraction of the time it would take to create them from scratch. A single, centralized process to check all incarcerations in a state or its counties can help multiple programs validate that payments are not being inappropriately made to people in prison or jail. Common data can be used, within the approved governance structure, for multiple business purposes.

Repeat and reuse is an excellent way to gain synergy and efficiency across analytic solutions—but be cautious to avoid being lulled into a mindset of been there, done that. While we want to bring new analytic solutions to value as quickly and effectively as possible, always consider innovation and creativity in your solution—is there room to improve an existing component, expand an existing dataset, or enhance how we use our tools? Transformation in government should never stall because that's how we've always done it.

## Technology

Data management and analytics technology provide the tools to bring data together and help our government users understand the key information that impacts their business decisions and activities. In the past, analytics tools were seen as complicated, backroom utilities, used only by researchers, statisticians, and data scientists. While those highly technical capabilities are still central to in-depth, advanced analysis, technology has evolved. New tools are more intuitive and user friendly, allowing user communities to access their data and perform their own analysis. Data visualization and executive dashboards provide quick insights with the ability to dig into the details. A COA can leverage common technology platforms to ensure the right tools are used for the right purposes—building expertise and knowledge of tools, providing a consistent analytic experience to their user community and ensuring that data is accessible to the business users who need it.

## BUILDING A CENTER OF ANALYTICS?

Now I recognize the value of a COA—that it can help my government gain a more complete understanding and to be able to see changes, trends, and issues associated with citizens, services, operational and program costs, and more at the enterprise level. I can see the value of stronger collaboration among my business units and IT, improved data management, greater analytics insights, and greater efficiency in building analytic solutions. But where do I start?

Enterprise programs, especially in government organizations, are often viewed as conceptual, bureaucratic, and rarely effective approaches. Even with the best intentions, the vision for implementing a COA can seem complex and overwhelming. It can be difficult to establish policy, procedures, engagement, and support when outcomes and results are theoretical. For the greatest success in cultivating a successful COA, *think big, start small*. Create a high-level vision that recognizes the value of enterprise data management, standard policies, and procedures, common tools and technology, and repeatable, efficient development process. But begin with a clearly defined scope that can rapidly prove the approach and show the value of analytics. While my state's program outlined a vision for enterprise data sharing and analytics, the compelling need for an enterprise criminal justice system helped our team define a clear scope, timeline, and deliverables that would show success quickly, build the framework for governance and management of the program, and help us learn how to expand across business areas. With that initial start, we grew into other areas with fraud analysis, always reusing and refining the way we managed data and the approach we used to build new solutions. This incremental approach enabled repeatable, successful implementations in many areas across our government.

To ensure support, commitment of resources, funding, and adoption, you must know the business issue. When we identify and focus on a compelling event—the rapidly growing opioid and heroin crisis, death and maltreatment of children in foster care, increasing Medicaid costs, or fraud in our revenue systems—we can define a scope of work with clear expectations and measureable outcomes. We can understand and engage the key stakeholders to be sure that the data and analytics results developed provide a solution that is relevant now and in the future.

Most importantly, we have to *make the journey iterative*. As we complete each analytic solution, we have the opportunity to review, evaluate, and enhance policy, procedure, and development activities. As we repeat, refine, and learn from each effort we can build best practices that evolve over time to improve efficiencies and bring solutions to value more quickly and at lower cost.

Government is accountable for the security and well-being of its citizens. Government has the data to ask questions, assess situations, shape our understanding, and inform our actions and decisions. A Center of Analytics can help government take a strategic, enterprise approach to managing its data and the analytics needed to enhance and optimize our business decisions.

**PROFILE**

**Kay Meyer** is principal industry consultant for state and local government at SAS Institute. She led in establishing and expanding North Carolina's enterprise Government Data Analytics Center, helping transform the state's analytic approach in criminal justice, fraud, waste, and compliance, and more. Meyer helps government meet key business challenges through the use of data and analytics with an enterprise vision. She received a BS from the University of Virginia and an MBA from George Washington University.

## NOTES

1. "Insights From the 2017 CIO Agenda Report: Seize the Digital Ecosystem Opportunity," Gartner Executive Programs (2016). www.gartner.com/imagesrv/cio/pdf/Gartner_CIO_Agenda_2017.pdf.

2. City of Boston Analytics Team, https://www.boston.gov/departments/analytics-team.

3. NYC Analytics, www1.nyc.gov/site/analytics/index.page.

4. H.R. 3103—104th Congress: Health Insurance Portability and Accountability Act of 1996, GovTrack.us (2016), https://www.govtrack.us/congress/bills/104/hr3103.

5. Publication 1075—Tax Information Security Guidelines for Federal, State, and Local Agencies, Safeguards for Protecting Federal Tax Returns and Return Information, https://www.irs.gov/pub/irs-pdf/p1075.pdf.

6. Family Educational Rights and Privacy Act; Final Rule, 34 CFR Part 99, Department of Education, https://www2.ed.gov/legislation/FedRegister/finrule/2004-2/042104a.pdf.

7. CJIS Information Security Officer, "Criminal Justice Information Services Security Policy, Version 5.5," Federal Bureau of Investigation (June 1, 2016), https://www.fbi.gov/services/cjis/cjis-security-policy-resource-center.

# Appendix

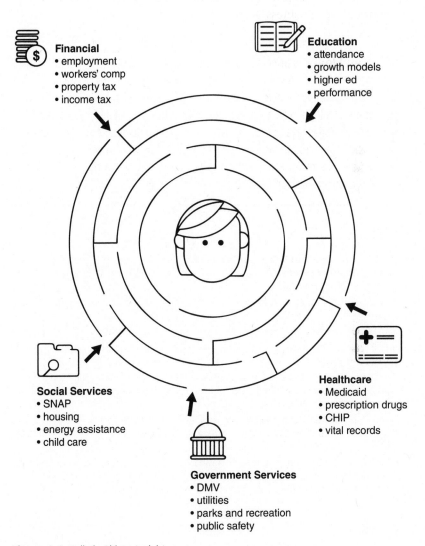

**Financial**
- employment
- workers' comp
- property tax
- income tax

**Education**
- attendance
- growth models
- higher ed
- performance

**Social Services**
- SNAP
- housing
- energy assistance
- child care

**Healthcare**
- Medicaid
- prescription drugs
- CHIP
- vital records

**Government Services**
- DMV
- utilities
- parks and recreation
- public safety

**Figure A.1** Holistic Citizen Insight.

# Index